IT ALL
STARTED WITH
FRESHMAN
ENGLISH

BOOKS BY RICHARD ARMOUR

Biography and Literary Criticism
Barry Cornwall: A Biography of Bryan Waller Procter
The Literary Recollections of Barry Cornwall
Coleridge the Talker (with Raymond F. Howes)

Play
To These Dark Steps (with Bown Adams)

Light Verse
All in Sport
An Armoury of Light Verse
For Partly Proud Parents
Golf Bawls
Leading with My Left
Light Armour
The Medical Muse
Nights with Armour
Privates' Lives
Punctured Poems
Yours for the Asking

Prose Humor and Satire
American Lit Relit
Armour's Almanac
The Classics Reclassified
A Diabolical Dictionary of Education

IT ALL STARTED WITH FRESHMAN ENGLISH

A survival kit for
students and teachers
of English and
a relaxed review
for those who are
happily past it all

by
RICHARD ARMOUR

McGraw-Hill Book Company
New York   Toronto   St. Louis
Düsseldorf   Mexico   Panama

Copyright © 1973 by Richard Armour.
All rights reserved.
Printed in the United States of America.
No part of this publication may be reproduced, stored
in a retrieval system or transmitted in any form or by
any means, electronic, mechanical, photocopying,
recording or otherwise, without the prior written
permission of the publisher.

First edition¡

Library of Congress Cataloging in Publication Data

Armour, Richard Willard, date
  It all started with freshman English.

  In part adapted from the author's English lit relit and
American lit relit.
  1. English literature—Anecdotes, facetiae, satire, etc.
  2. American literature—Anecdotes, facetiae, satire, etc.
  I. Title.
PR86.A72   820'.2'07   73-461
ISBN 0-07-002301-8

ACKNOWLEDGMENTS

Along with new material, not before published, this book brings together and occasionally condenses some of the light verse and playful prose I have written over the years about English and American literature, writing, teaching, and the academic life. Often I have found it more difficult to select and arrange and interweave than it was to write the original pieces.

Because of the mixture of old and new, because also of the many books (all of them my own) I have drawn upon, acknowledgments could become complicated, but I shall try to keep them simple. Before coming to my books of parody and spoofing of literature I must, however, give thanks for the use of my "At Random" and "Reading Habits of the Young," both from Martin Levin's "The Phoenix Nest," *Saturday Review.* Though not included in any of my books on literature and writing, these will be found, with appropriate Afterthoughts, in *Out of My Mind,* a collection of my short prose writings from many magazines.

The rest of the book consists of either previously unpublished material or tidbits (or just plain bits) from my books of light verse and my irreverent works on literature, all published by McGraw-Hill. To help identify the pieces with the books in which they first appeared, I am listing them by chapters and in the order in which the reader will encounter them. It may be assumed that whatever is not listed has never before been published. Here is what has appeared and where:

CHAPTER I. "Lines Long After Pope, by a Reader of Freshman Themes" and "Survey of the Romantic Poets," *Light Armour;* "A Nightmare of Undigested Reading of the Poets," *Nights with Armour.*

CHAPTER II. "Disclosure," *Light Armour;* "The Split Infinitive" and "Punctuation Remarks," *Nights with Armour;* "The Comma," "The Colon," and "The Exclamation Mark (Point)," *On Your Marks: A Package of Punctuation.*

CHAPTER III. A portion, condensed, of *English Lit Relit.*

CHAPTER IV. "Hamlet," *Twisted Tales from Shakespeare.*

CHAPTER V. "David Copperfield," *The Classics Reclassified.*

CHAPTER VI. Longfellow, Henley, and Tennyson parodies, from "The Poets Revisited," *Nights with Armour;* sample couplets from *Punctured Poems: Famous First and Infamous Second Lines* (first published by Prentice-Hall, 1966).

CHAPTER VII. A portion, condensed, of *American Lit Relit.*

CHAPTER VIII. "The Scarlet Letter," *The Classics Reclassified.*

CHAPTER IX. "Dean of the Faculty," *Going Around in Academic Circles;* definitions of "Curriculum" and "Department," *A Diabolical Dictionary of Education* (first published by World Publishing Company, 1969); "Department Head" and "Professor's Progress," *Going Around in Academic Circles.*

I should like to bow deeply to the dean of American literary agents, my own agent and good friend, Paul R. Reynolds, for giving me the idea for this book and for insisting that I write it. Finally, I thank my editor at McGraw-Hill, Lou Ashworth, for encouragement, critical help, and, above all, answering my letters.

R.A.

Contents

IT ALL
STARTED WITH
FRESHMAN
ENGLISH

I

It All Started with Freshman English

When I started teaching, I carried the normal load (as we say in the trade) of four sections of Freshman English, with thirty students in each. That was at the University of Texas in 1928. One of my classes met Monday, Wednesday, and Friday at 8:00 A.M. and one on Tuesday, Thursday, and Saturday at 8:00 A.M.—in other words, before my students were fully awake. The third class met at 11:00 A.M., when they were getting hungry, while the fourth met just after lunch, when they were getting sleepy.

My 120 students wrote a theme each week, on some such subject as "What I Did Last Summer" or "Why I Came to College." I read each paper carefully and wrote comments that filled the margins. I also gave frequent quizzes. Since I had to remain in the room to see that there was no cheating, I had a good chance to size up the girls in the class, who were busy writing or who pursed their lips prettily while thinking.

In addition, I kept my office hours faithfully, in a small room I shared with two other young instructors. There I was kept busy justifying my grades (I had been told the

Department Chairman liked hard graders) to students who thought they had been treated unfairly.

I was trying to earn my salary of $1800.

Many years later, looking back on those four sections of Freshman English, I wrote this couplet:

**LINES LONG AFTER POPE,
BY A READER OF FRESHMAN THEMES**

Small wit is theirs, in shopworn phrases dressed;
What oft was thought, and twice as well expressed.

I was a serious, somewhat frightened young man, trained for the teaching of Freshman English by the arduous study of Old English, Middle English, Middle English dialects, Gothic, Old French, Old Norse, and Indo-European philology. This was accomplished at Harvard, where the English department of the graduate school was dominated by professors who had studied in Germany and thought their students should suffer as much as they had suffered. At any rate, anyone taking a Ph.D. in English should be well grounded in such things as Grimm's Law, or *Lautverschiebungen,* and the Saxon patois of the Blickling Homilies.

As I went onward to other colleges and universities and upward from teaching Freshman English to teaching English and American literature, I found it difficult to apply my Gothic to a course in Shakespeare and my Old Norse to Contemporary Poets. Even in Creative Writing I was hard pressed to make use of my knowledge of such things as umlaut, ablaut, and *Aktionsart.* But I tried.

For almost forty years I taught at a wide variety of institutions. I was forever on the move, looking for better pay and better students. At some point, I am not sure precisely when, I developed my Reasons for Teaching English. Though they should be carved in marble, I set them down here:

1. English is better than Chemistry, since an incorrect mixture of authors will not blow you up.

2. English is better than Mathematics, especially if you like classroom discussion and writing critical comments on papers.

3. English is better than Art, because you can read Milton, or even Faulkner, without getting paint under your fingernails.

4. English is better than Music, or at least Violin, because the book you suddenly decide to read aloud from in class doesn't have a broken string.

5. English is almost as good as Biology if you get a kick out of discussing sex in the classroom.

6. English gives you an excuse for reading books you want to read anyhow, and you can get free copies from the publishers if you lie a little about making them required, or even collateral, reading.

7. Biography is a legitimate part of English, and great authors are almost as interesting oddballs as great artists and great musicians.

8. English is better than History, Philosophy, Psychology, Religion, Political Science, and Sociology, because all of these can be worked into the teaching of English without running the risk of giving offense politically or ideologically to parents, trustees, and alumni.

9. Teaching English, in fact teaching anything, is better than working.

10. Once you discover parody and are willing to be a little irreverent about books and writers you really love, and once you learn how good it feels to have students laughing with you instead of at you, English is better than

3

anything. Anything, that is, you are likely to do in a classroom.

These Reasons for Teaching English are not listed in order of importance. Nor are they listed in chronological order. It happens that the tenth Reason, which I came upon last, is the one I would place first. At any rate it is the one that helped me most and that I eventually did the most about. I was becoming aware of it, I now realize, while giving a course in the Romantic Poets. I wrote the following lines, which I read to my students at the end of the last class, just before I gathered up my books and notes and walked out.

SURVEY OF THE ROMANTIC POETS

Wordsworth, who was fairly mild,
Had an illegitimate child.
Coleridge almost all his life
Yearned for someone not his wife.
Shelley, an amoral elf,
Caused his wife to drown herself.
Byron, who was most tempestuous,
Went the limit, was incestuous.
Keats, who might have had the gumption,
Was retarded by consumption.
Rarely did the great Romantics
Equal, in their verse, their antics.

I justified these lines as a condensation and review of the five poets we studied in the course. But I am not sure any such justification was necessary. The students seemed to enjoy this bit of verse and to like me a little better for being willing to have some fun with writers I had been telling them all year were among the greatest. Wordsworth I had had a little trouble selling—until I got into the

4

matter of his illegitimate daughter. If something of the sort could be turned up about Tennyson, even that poet would be easier to teach. Writers of articles for the scholarly journals are still working on it and hoping, but it seems unlikely that anything scandalous will be discovered at this late date.

Let me point out that I read those lines about the Romantic Poets at the *end* of the course, not the beginning. Disrespectful and irreverent as I may seem to be, I think authors and their works should be given to students straight the first time around. A teacher owes this to the author and to the student. Besides, the student must know a novel, play, or poem, and know it well, before being able to understand and enjoy a lighthearted, playful approach to it.

Once I wrote a piece of verse that weaves together, with sly distortions, more than thirty well-known lines or phrases by poets from Shakespeare to T. S. Eliot. A student who can identify all of the quotations has probably done well in the Survey Course or has a good if somewhat erratic memory.

A NIGHTMARE OF UNDIGESTED
READING OF THE POETS

When I have fears that I may cease to bleed
Upon the thorns of life, I am a weed
(Yet fortune helps the brave deserve the fair)
Whose name is writ in water everywhere
Nor any drop to drink. Grow old along
With me, for I can give thee but a song
Sung by an idiot boy. Not so unkind
As man's ingratitude to man, my mind
A kingdom is: I've loved thee, Cinema,
Not wisely but too well. I also saw,

5

When I was one and twenty, Shelley plain,
Far from the madding crowd's ignoble stain
On the white radiance of eternity.
Tripping the light fantastic o'er the lea,
Much have I traveled in the realms of cold
And wrapped my threadbare cloak about,
    though old
And with a ravelled sleave of care that sleep,
Perchance to dream, and sorrow's crown too
    deep
For tears, might mend. If winter comes, can
    spring
Be far behind a young man's fancy? Sing
Cuccu! Cuccu! Poor Tom's a-cold and June's
Still far, and measured out with coffee spoons.

How crazy can I get? A little crazier than that some-times. Mostly, however, at least in the classroom and in what I write for use in the classroom, there is method in my madness, or madness in my method. A parody of an author is, or can be, a form of literary criticism. Humor is sometimes the glue that sticks facts to the mind. I have had letters from students who thanked me for helping them answer questions on a test. They said they remem-bered something from one of my tongue-in-cheek books rather than from their textbook. Since my memory is deteriorating more rapidly each year, I must read one of my books myself.

Of course my motive for writing as I do may be that I am envious of the writers I fool around with, and I am trying to pull them down to my own level. I hope this is not true, but I feel better now that I have confessed the possibility. Though "Trees" is hardly a great poem, I once wrote this couplet about it:

JOYCE KILMER REVISITED

I'd rather far have written "Trees"
Than all its thousand parodies.

If I feel that way about "Trees," imagine how I feel about *David Copperfield* and *Hamlet*, to mention only two of the works I have irreverently retold. Before I leave "Trees," though, let me add that of all the parodies of this much-parodied poem I most admire and envy the famous one by Ogden Nash, in which he expresses the fear that unless the billboards fall, "I'll never see a tree at all."

Though I have taught just about every author and period and literary type in English and American literature, my specialties have been the Romantic Poets, Milton, and Chaucer. The Romantic Poets I have already mentioned. I wrote three publish-or-perish books on them and am grateful to these authors for keeping me from perishing and for moving me up to a full professorship. It occurs to me that if we have a full professor, why shouldn't an associate professor be a half-full professor and an assistant professor a quarter-full professor? What professors are full of I shall not go into here.

Milton led me to my greatest literary disaster. I collaborated with a professional playright on a three-act play based on Milton's life. It had everything in it (i.e., too much): the poet's blindness, his three wives, and the Great Fire of 1666. There was an experimental playing of it in New York, and it had a magnificent run of one night. Though I retired forthwith as a dramatist, I was generously permitted to continue teaching my course in Milton and the Seventeenth Century.

As for Chaucer, he is my favorite of favorites. I taught Chaucer for more than thirty years to graduate and undergraduate students, and named our son after him. Our son

7

has never appreciated this, since he is frequently called "Guffrey" and "Gee-o-free," but my intentions were good. What I like best about Chaucer is his understanding of the human race. As Kittredge has said of him: "His specialty was mankind." If he were in graduate school today, he would have to narrow his field considerably.

One of my fondest wishes is to call Chaucer up (or down) from wherever he is and have about five minutes with him. I would like to have him read some of the Prologue to *The Canterbury Tales* into a tape recorder. It would settle a few arguments about pronunciation, and I hope I have been right all these years.

One more word about Chaucer. He tells us that the Clerk of Oxenford would gladly learn and gladly teach. By "gladly" I like to think he meant cheerfully, happily, enthusiastically. It must have been harder for the Clerk than for some of us, because his field was Philosophy rather than English.

As for me, I would expand "gladly" to include "playfully." Not every day, but now and then, especially on the dark days. Some years ago I spoke at a meeting of the California Association of Teachers of English. Subsequently these English teachers brought out in their journal a selection of my prose and light verse that they called "Richard Armour Lightens the Load." Remembering the load I once carried, now no longer on my shoulders or head or wherever, I decided to put together in one volume a sampling of what is intended to bring both lightness and light into the classroom.

But before coming to English and American literature, let us take a look at what is thought by some to be the greatest chore of all, and perhaps a complete waste of time—teaching students how to write.

II
Learning to Write

I believe in making an early start at writing, at least as early as high school. If a beginning can be made in kindergarten, so much the better. I did not write with the aim of being read until I was in college, and only a little then, for the campus paper and the humor magazine. The Freshman English course, then called Freshman Composition, was required (which is why I took it), a bore, and of no help. I got a "C plus" the first semester and pulled up to a "B" by the end of the year. What caused me to do that well was the instructor's inability to read my handwriting. He was humane enough to give me the benefit of the doubt about possible misspellings.

After college came that horrendous period in graduate school that set back my writing about ten years.

From first grade through graduate school I never had a teacher who helped me much with my writing. It was not until I married that I acquired a competent critic and proofreader. My wife, who is by nature a kind, gentle person, turns razor-sharp when she reads the first sentence of anything I have just written. She gave up teaching third grade to marry me, and my gain was her students' loss. It is good to have a seven-day-a-week resident critic, but I wish she had been my third-grade teacher. We were twenty-six when we married, and my bad habits, including bad writing habits, were by then deeply engrained.

I have said that I wrote for the campus paper when I was in college. I am always encouraging high school and college students to write for the school paper and enter every contest that comes along. It does something to you to see your writing in print. It may make you quit, then and there, but more likely it will give you the urge to write more and better. Unlike writing for a course, this is writing done of your own volition. I have known students who got an "A" in a writing course and then, after the last paper was handed in, never wrote again. Writing for the school paper (preferably a column rather than straight news reporting, though both are good) is a test not only of ability but of the will to keep at it. Writing with motives other than grades and academic credit comes close to what happens in what is called the "real world," except that there you get not only satisfaction but acceptances, rejections, and maybe a little money.

At the very least, writing for campus publications is a useful complement and supplement to the writing done for a course. If students will let them, teachers should occasionally write for these publications too. They will have to write better, or more clearly, than in their articles for the learned journals.

In this connection, teachers might also write some of the things they assign their students. When I joined the faculty of Wells College, in 1934, I took the place of Robert P. Tristram Coffin, the Maine poet. I soon learned from the students I inherited from him that he almost always wrote what he asked them to write. When they turned in their papers, he turned in his, or read it to the class. Once he assigned a poem on a certain topic and in a certain form and wrote to these specifications himself. I never found out whether the students graded him, but if

they did they should have given him an "A." What he
wrote turned out to be the leading poem in *Strange Holi-
ness,* the book for which he won the Pulitzer Prize in 1936.
See what you have been missing, teachers?

Can writing be taught? Some of it can: such things as
spelling, punctuation, sentence structure, paragraphing. A
teacher can point out wordiness, vagueness, repetition,
and other faults and can suggest improvements. Beyond
that, beyond the corrections and comments, the best thing
a teacher can do for students is to get them to read and
analyze good models and see how writers they admire do
it. Writing, like golf or acting or carpentering, is learned
by imitating the experts. Robert Louis Stevenson, you
remember, said he "played the sedulous ape." Good writers are usually good readers. Once I met a writer who told
me that every day, before he started writing, he read for
fifteen minutes in a little book called *The Beauties of
Shakespeare,* a selection of some of the best passages from
Shakespeare's works. "It tunes me up," he said. "It gives
my vocabulary a lift."

So a teacher can prod students into reading. Or, better,
lure them into reading. The teacher can read passages
aloud, with excitement and enthusiasm, and then the
teacher and students can discuss what is so good about
them. Together, for instance, they can try to figure out
what a writer does to catch the reader with that opening
sentence and how the writer keeps hold of the reader to
the last word of the last page. Catherine Drinker Bowen
says she has a sign over her desk that raises a question of
great importance to her and to any writer. The question
is: "Will the reader turn the page?"

Writing is almost impossible to teach all by itself. It
needs to be taught along with good examples, in other
words with literature. Once I took over a class that for
many years had been called "Freshman Composition." I

lost no time changing the title to "Introduction to Literature and Writing." The students, in turn, lost no time shortening it to "Lit and Writ." Each time we studied a literary work, the students wrote something of their own in the same form. When it was a novel or a play, they wrote only the opening or a portion of such a work.

I have also taught a course in "Advanced Writing" (a descriptive title I prefer to the usual "Creative Writing"), in which a few students managed to write, revise, and rewrite a complete novel. One wrote a novel that was published three years later. I can see it now, as I look up from my typewriter. It is on a nearby shelf in my study, in both hardcover and paperback editions. The author was a determined, hard-driving student, and I am happy to say that this was only the first of several books. One of them I had the additional satisfaction of reviewing—favorably, you may be sure.

If I were teaching a course in writing today, especially a beginning course, I know what I would do at the first meeting of the class. I would express the hope that every student had a typewriter and knew how to use it. By knowing how to use it, I mean not only being able to type but being able (and willing) to change a ribbon and clean the keys, notably the "p," "b," "a," "o," "d," "g," and "e." I am thinking of the teacher who has to read student papers, even as I am thinking of the joy of hitting keys and seeing the letters and words leap onto the white page. I dislike faint or fuzzy type almost as much as I dislike faint or fuzzy thoughts.

I wrote longhand all through school—high school, college, graduate school—and bought my first typewriter (secondhand, for twenty-five dollars) when I had to type my 800-page dissertation in triplicate and couldn't afford to have it typed by someone else. I had the help of a booklet, *How to Type in Ten Easy Lessons,* but mostly I learned by doing. When I finished typing that dissertation, I was a pretty fair typist. Now, forty years later, I am spectacular. True, I use only six fingers, but I cross one hand over the other like a piano virtuoso and make astonishing speed, as well as numerous typographical errors.

After making sure that every student had a typewriter or would have one as soon as finances permitted, I would proceed to what is at the very heart of writing: words. Within reach of that typewriter should be the writer's Bible, a dictionary, preferably one that is unabridged and up-to-date. Words are to a writer what stones are to a stonemason. They must be selected, fondled, fitted together to build the poem or story or article or play or book.

To a writer, there is more to words than their dictionary definition or their connotation. Words are not only long and short but light and heavy, smooth and rough. Coleridge once defined prose as "words in the best order" and poetry as "the best words in the best order." It helps the writer of prose if he also writes poetry, or at least reads it. In poetry, the individual word counts for more than in prose, and the shorter the poem the more this is true.

A mother once came to W. H. Auden and asked for his advice. She said she hoped her son would become a poet.

"Does he like ideas?" Auden asked.

"Yes," the mother said, "he does."

"Well, I don't know," Auden said. "But tell me, does he like words?"

"Oh, yes," the mother said, "he loves words."

"Then," said Auden, "there is a good chance he will become a poet."

I would go beyond Auden and say that love of words is the first requirement of a writer, either of poetry or of prose. Whether a love of words can be taught, I am not sure. But if the teacher is a word lover and keeps a dictionary in the classroom and occasionally tracks down the origin of a word and is always writing interesting words on the blackboard, it could happen. If the students don't come to love words, they may come to love the teacher.

Before I leave Auden, let me quote what he once wrote about the way words shape the writer's thinking, especially the poet's. In his *Poets at Work,* Auden asks this provocative question: "How can I know what I think till I see what I say?" His question led me to write these lines:

DISCLOSURE

How could the poet
possibly know
till the very last word
in the very last row?

For a poem's a word
plus a word plus a word,
added, subtracted,
and thoroughly stirred.

And thought makes the word
and the word makes thought,
and some things come
that were never sought.

At what he has said
when his say is done,
the poet's surprised
as anyone.

The teacher, hoping to develop an interest in words, might even try a pun now and then, first explaining that a pun is an ancient and honorable device, a play on words, that was used (sometimes brilliantly and sometimes none too well) by Shakespeare and Charles Lamb, among others, and can be found also in the writings of such respected moderns as Vladimir Nabokov and John Updike. If that is not enough to give dignity to the pun, the teacher could add that the word comes from the Italian *puntiglio,* a quibble or fine point, and has the same root as "punctilious"; that if you don't like the word "pun" you can use the more impressive sounding "paronomasia"; that the pun is used throughout the world, in Germany being called *Wortspiel* and in France *jeu de mot;* and that a bad pun is a pun made by someone else.

But now, to call attention to words and to bring a little fun into that writing class, let me introduce a game I myself play and have suggested (or required) students to play. Here it is:

AT RANDOM

The other day I opened my dictionary at random. I wasn't looking up the word "random," but it just happened to open there. If it hadn't, however, I would never have known about "randem," which is an adjective describing three horses harnessed to a vehicle, one behind the other. That is one more than you usually have in a tandem. I hope soon to find occasion to use the word, though if I use it in speech it will be taken for a mispronunciation and if I use it in writing it will be thought a misspelling. As I long ago discovered, not only a little learning but too much learning is a dangerous thing.

However my discovery of "randem" led me to start flipping the dictionary open again and again, as if spinning the wheel at a gambling casino. It was not only pure chance but pure fun. I couldn't lose anything more than a little time, or perhaps a fingernail.

The first slip of the pages led me to "slubberdegullion."

This is defined as a mean wretch, a base, slovenly boor. I have been saying it over and over, and find it rolls nicely off the tongue. Moreover, I shall probably find a use for it sooner than for "random," since I am rarely around horses but know a couple of slubberdegullions. I plan to use the word the first time I am around either of them, but not too loudly since both slubberdegullions are bigger than I am.

Another turn of the pages, this time toward the front, and I found a word that may, in this day of women's rights, be just what we need. The word is "alderwoman," which is defined as a woman who is an alderman. I had thought that a woman who is an alderman would be called an aldermaness, but an aldermaness, I find, is not a female alderman but the wife of an alderman. Awareness of this will spare me considerable embarrassment if I am ever in the presence of an alderman, the wife of an alderman, or an alderwoman. I shall also be careful to pronounce "alderwoman" so that it doesn't sound like "older woman."

Next I turned toward the back of the dictionary and hit pay dirt the very first time. It was the word "wedbed" that caught my eye. A wedbed is the same as a marriage bed, and seems to me better because it not only saves a syllable but rhymes within itself, and very few words have this poetic quality. Delighted as I was with wedbed, I was even happier with the word immediately below it, "wedbedrip."

A wedbedrip, I supposed, is a rip-roaring time on the wedding night. Actually a wedbedrip is an old legal term in England meaning "a covenant by which a tenant was bound to do bedrip for his lord." The tenant would rip a bed apart, I conjectured, just to please his sadistic master or to show his brute strength. Wrong again. Turning to the front of the dictionary once more, I found "bedrip" to be a day's reaping—in feudal times a service due from a tenant at his lord's request.

My game of opening the dictionary at random promises many happy hours and precious rewards. Since my dictionary has 3210 three-column pages, it should last me through many a long, hard winter. Moreover, if anyone calls me a slubberdegullion I'll know what he means. But he may not know what I mean when I tell him he's let himself in for a week of bedrip.

I am suggesting this dictionary game as a way of bringing some playfulness as well as word lore into a writing course. Students could be asked to bring to class and talk about the most unusual words they have uncovered while flipping back and forth through the dictionary. I tried this out while taking over a writing class at a college I was visiting, with the instructor sitting in the back of the room. At the next meeting of the class I found that the students, playing my dictionary game, had turned up some rare words indeed, but the one who had worked hardest at it and had unearthed or undictionaried the oddest and most interesting words was the instructor. We had a great hour of fun with words, and I like to think some vocabularies were enlarged. I know mine was.

Outside the classroom I have discovered another use for the game or an offshoot of it, which involves pursuing a word through the eleven-volume *New English Dictionary*. This led me, for instance, to write an article on the word "medicine" for *The Journal of the American Medical Association*. I told the medical profession about such things as "medicaster," a term used in the seventeenth century for a pretender to medical skill whom we would today call a "quack," and the "medicinable ring" once worn by physicians on what came to be known as the "medicinable finger." The medicinable ring was blessed by a priest, or even by the Pope, and was supposed to have special curative powers.

Working with etymology rather than history, I once wrote an article for *Parents' Magazine* in which I explained that the word "father" is related not only to "patrician" and "patriot" but to "Jupiter." That is something I doubt many fathers, or their children, are aware of. It raised my own status in our family, at least for a few minutes, when I pointed it out.

But it isn't necessary to become involved in etymology or the history of the language. Let me give you an example of what can be done with a simple, ordinary word, the word "half."

NOT EVEN HALF TRYING

The other day I found myself saying, "Half a loaf is better than none." I had never before given much thought to this aphorism, but I was suddenly filled with a desire to know more. The first thing I wondered about was where this old saying comes from. It was easy enough to trace it to John Heywood's *Proverbes,* first printed in 1546, in which it appears as "Better is halfe a lofe than no bread." It probably had been around, orally, for a long time before that. But what I still wondered about is why it isn't "a quarter of a loaf" or "an eighth of a loaf" or some other modest portion.

This led me, still wondering, to wonder about our fixation on "half." Sticking with that loaf of bread for a moment, I wonder why, when a loaf is partly eaten, we say it is half-eaten. Never, or rarely, a third or a fifth eaten. Though I am not much good at mathematics, this seems to me sloppy or at least inexact.

In the same way, a person who is neither fully clothed nor naked is half-clad and not a tenth clad or whatever. A door is either open, closed, or half-closed. True, it is sometimes ajar, which I gather is somewhat less than half-closed or, for that matter, half-open. When eating at a restaurant, I have often heard my wife say that the food was half-cooked and if I were half a man I'd summon the waiter and tell him to send it back to the kitchen. Did I say my wife? I mean my better half. Anyhow, half-starved and only half listening, I eat what is put before me.

This is serious business. At least I am half-serious about it. I am only half joking. Sometimes, I confess, I have been guilty of a half-truth, which many consider worse, or at least trickier, than an outright lie. I also occasionally have a half-baked idea at night when I am half-asleep, perhaps kept awake by a half-digested dish of a half-dozen oysters on the half shell. I have lain there in the half light of dawn, thinking I should get up and take some bicarbonate of soda, but half-afraid of waking my wife.

In the morning I get up, half-dead from lack of sleep, and draw on my half-calf socks, still alert enough to quote, half-jokingly, Tennyson's "Half a league, half a league" (or should it be "half a leg, half a leg?") "half a league onward." Halfway through breakfast, sipping my coffee with its half-and-half and eating my cereal, onto which I have poured half half-and-half and half milk, I think of George Herbert's "Half the world knows not how the other half lives," and am half ashamed that I live so well, when many in the world are half-starved.

"You've left half your cereal," my wife says, half-annoyed, but I hurry out, half running, knowing I'm half an hour late.

Halfheartedly setting off for work, my eyes still half-closed and my brain only half functioning, I think of things like half measures, half-forgotten promises, half pay, half gainers, half nelsons, halfbacks, half cousins, half time, and time-and-a-half. Call me half-wit if you will. As John Heywood didn't say, but as he might have said if he had been even half thinking, "Half a wit is better than none."

Words, then, come first, and if a course in writing does no more than develop an interest in words, it has probably been worth the time and effort. But in an introductory course there are some matters of mechanics and usage that cannot be sidestepped, even if the word "grammar" is never mentioned.

Consider the split infinitive. There is a good deal of argument about whether an infinitive should occasionally, rarely, or never be split. In *The Careful Writer,* one of my favorite books about modern English usage, Theodore Bernstein devotes two and a half pages to the split infinitive, avoidance of which he calls an unreasonable taboo and yet "a linguistic fact of life." In short, unless it would be ambiguous or clumsy to do otherwise, he would *not* split an infinitive. His reason is that as long as the unsplit infinitive is the norm, to split an infinitive would irritate and distract too many readers. There is a changing attitude toward the split infinitive, and according to Bernstein, who is the authority on such things for *The New York Times,* in fifty years it may be acceptable. But not just now.

Many years ago I wrote these lines:

THE SPLIT INFINITIVE

The split infinitive not only splits
Infinitives but people. Plainly it's

Responsible for making a division
Into three sorts: he who, with fine derision,
Looks down his nose at vulgar splitters; he
Who, knowing better, splits defiantly
And scorns the pedant and perfectionist;
And he, the very bottom of the list,
And yet by far the happiest, who lives
In ignorance of split infinitives.

Of course the writer cannot be in the last category. Ignorance is not bliss for him. He must know what a split infinitive is and the risk he is taking if he decides, for the sake of clarity, to use one rather than get around it by writing a whole new sentence that hasn't an infinitive, split or unsplit, in it.

I hope you noticed my faulty parallelism in the opening lines of "The Split Infinitive." I know it should be "splits not only" instead of "not only splits," but I was boxed into this by exigencies of rhyme and meter. Forgive me. I'll try not to do it again.

One more look at the split infinitive, before I reluctantly move on to other matters:

SPLITTING HEADACHE

To carelessly and wrongly split
Infinitives I must admit
I've tried to very rarely do.
To ever split was bad, I knew.
But now I want to in my way
And simply and directly say
That once you try to really plan
To always split them when you can—
To not avoid but work for one—
It gets to somehow seem like fun.

21

If there is one thing that perplexes student writers, in fact all writers, more than anything else, it is punctuation. You can lose a friend (especially a fellow English teacher) if he or she happens to punctuate a series a, b and c, while you are a little too insistent that it should be a, b, and c. I happen to be of the a, b, and c school, because this punctuation avoids ambiguity. I would not give my life, or even my wife, for that second comma, but I can get worked up about it and might even come to blows over it if the a, b and c person is nasty, persistent, and smaller than I am. (Notice my punctuation of "nasty, persistent, and smaller.")

Punctuation and words go together. It is hard to believe that once, in early manuscripts, there were no punctuation marks to help the reader. Then along came dots to keep sentences apart. And now we have, and should be grateful for, sixteen marks, each with its special and very useful function. One of these days there may be seventeen, if the interrobang, that ingenious combination of the question mark and the exclamation point, is generally accepted.

Once I read a book review in which the reviewer became a little too enthusiastic about the book he was reviewing. "Even the commas are entertaining!" he exclaimed, properly using an exclamation point. Taking off from this, I wrote the following lines:

PUNCTUATION REMARKS

Admiringly we must admit
This is the apogee of wit,
When commas (though it's not made plain
Just how it's done) can entertain.

It might perhaps be how absurd
They look, head bent behind a word

And tail tucked like a scolded dog's,
These punctuation polliwogs.

But let us not neglect, while grinning
At clowning commas, squirming, chinning,
The semicolons, holding poses
Like seals, with balls upon their noses,

And dashes—dashing, lean, and narrow—
For bow-parentheses an arrow,
And lynx-eyed colons, coldly peering,
And quotes, cheerleaders jumping, cheering,

And question marks, small shepherd crooks
That bring a rustic touch to books,
Each balanced on a small black ball. . . .
What fun! Why read the words at all?

I made use of this in a talk I gave to a group of English teachers. When I finished, a teacher who had been in the audience came up to me and shook my hand. I am always pleased when an English teacher shakes my hand instead of his fist. Of course the teacher may be softening me up a little before telling me of some word I have mispronounced.

In this instance the English teacher not only shook my hand but did the best thing anyone can do for me. He gave me an idea for a book.

"I liked that poem you read," he said. "Why don't you write a whole book about the punctuation marks? Have some fun with them. I could use such a book in my class."

There, I could see, was a person of taste and discernment, a stimulating, creative teacher. Anyone who not only gives me an idea for a book but says he will use it in his class, perhaps even requiring his students to buy a copy, is my friend for life.

As soon as I could get to my typewriter I started to work. The result of the English teacher's suggestion and my putting words together was *On Your Marks: A Package of Punctuation.* Ogden Nash, who at first said, "I have an ironclad rule never to write a foreword or introduction," asked to have a look at the manuscript anyhow. He wrote back, "It's delightful. I'll write the foreword." This he did, within two weeks, and I jubilantly wrote him, "You've written the best page in the book!"

On Your Marks: A Package of Punctuation is a playful treatment in verse of the period, comma, semicolon, colon, question mark, exclamation mark (point), quotation marks, parentheses, brackets, dash, hyphen, apostrophe, underlining, asterisk, caret, and ellipsis. I dedicated it to Aldus Manutius (1450–1515), the Venetian printer and founder of the Aldine press who regularized the use of the various punctuation marks. I call him "the father of modern punctuation," and have the evidence to prove it, though his contributions in this field, except for invention of italic type, have largely been overlooked.

In my little book I didn't go into the details of punctuation and sentence structure. Such matters I left to the many handbooks on the subject. My aim, once again, was to bring some fun into what is usually one of the dullest parts of studying or teaching English. In playful verse, and using excessively the punctuation mark I happened to be describing, I tried to make each mark lively and alive, not an enemy but a helpful friend.

The book can be used as early as third or fourth grade, and from then on through high school. There are college students who tell me they have enjoyed it and even learned a few things from it, for instance what the ellipsis is and why you sometimes use three dots and sometimes four.

Here are three of the punctuation marks as I see them:

THE COMMA

Consider the comma, most used of all marks.
In back of a word,
You will notice,
It parks
And waits for the reader and tells him to pause
Before, let us say,
He begins a new clause.

Its head on the line and its tail hanging down,
It looks like a polliwog trailing a noun,
And, having no arms,
There it clings by its chin,
Amidst the fat words looking tiny and thin.

Yet small though it is,
It shows lion-like heart
In keeping two parts of a sentence apart
And helping the reader, down wordways ca-
    reening,
Get just the right emphasis,
Just the right meaning.

It doesn't say, "Stop!"
It says, "Caution" or "Slow,"
And that can be very important, you know.

THE COLON

The colon by some is thought odd,
And no wonder:
Two periods make it,
One over,
One under.

104569

The colon resembles the eyes of a beast:
A tiger,
A fox,
Or a tomcat at least—
Two eyes ever looking, two eyes open wide,
That belong to a creature that lies on its side.

Unable to point or to say, "Over there,"
All the colon can do,
And it does it,
Is stare.
So here's a suggestion: go on, if you please,
To where it is looking, to see what it sees.

THE EXCLAMATION MARK (POINT)

Wham!
Bang!
Zowie!
Oh!
Here is a mark it's exciting to know.
If it's called not a mark but a point, this is why!
It points like a rocket right up at the sky,
A rocket just launched from its pad with a blast
And a *swish!* and a *swoosh!*
And it's rising fast!

It's slim
And it's trim
And it's soldier straight,
Like a guard that's on guard at a palace gate.
It's also like someone set free who was bound,
Now joyfully jumping a foot off the ground.

You find it with grim and you find it with gay,
Not only with "Ouch!"
But, as often, "Hooray!"

It's not for a whisper, it's more for a shout,
So look for excitement when it is about!

My first and probably last experience with film making
was adapting *On Your Marks* for the animated film of
that name, narrated by Herschel Bernardi and released by
Communications Group West in Hollywood. Since it was
decided to make it in two parts, putting the eight easier
marks in the first part, for use in elementary schools, and
the eight more difficult marks in the second part, for use
in junior high schools and high schools, I had to write new
introductory and concluding sections and make other
changes. Also I wrote a little story in prose, about a boy
and a girl who visit a zoo, into which the punctuation
marks could insert themselves. This might seem easy, but
it was as difficult a thing, per word, as I have ever written.
The first sentence had to have a period and no other
punctuation. The second sentence had to have a comma.
The third had to have a colon. And so on. Try it sometime.

As one who has rarely won a prize for anything, even at
a county fair, I was pleased when the film of *On Your
Marks* won second place for educational films at the
American Film Festival. I don't remember what film won
first place, and I don't want to. I am made jealous very
easily.

I wish I had been taught early in life to write simply,
directly. No teacher ever scolded me or graded me down
for writing complicated, involved sentences. No teacher
ever suggested that I break some of my sentences, almost
ready to break of their own weight, into two or even three.

I was a wordy, roundabout writer until I was in my late
thirties. My sentences were a maze of subordinate clauses
and parentheses. I still have trouble ending one sentence

and starting another, but I have improved. Who, or what, helped me? The Army.

After serving with troops for two years in World War II, I was rescued by a general whose aide I had been. He took me with him to the War Department General Staff. It was the luckiest thing that ever happened to me. Not only was I snug and safe, with nothing more dangerous to contend with than a typewriter, but during my last year in the Pentagon I became involved in ghostwriting for several high-ranking generals, including the Chief of Staff.

The help to my writing came in three ways. First, what I wrote was revised by aides and by the General himself, and I received a copy of what was finally used: a report, speech, letter, or whatever. Invariably, I found that what I had written had been improved. Among other things, there was usually a pruning, a removing of the repetitious and the unnecessary. Time after time I asked myself, "Why didn't *I* write it that way?" Of course the General had a little advantage in knowing what it was he wanted to say.

Second, and very nearly as important, I had an inflexible deadline. Chief of Staff papers had to be written (and approved by other staff members and checked and revised) within twenty-four hours. That, at any rate, was the average time allowed, and a chart was kept of the performance of each Division. I was in the G-3 Division, otherwise known as Plans and Training. Having a deadline forced me into simplicity and directness. I had no time for extra words, words which would probably be removed anyhow.

The third way my Army experience helped my writing was by making me write, write, write. I wrote from morning till night, six and sometimes seven days a week. I wrote on a wide variety of subjects, the Army at the General Staff level being involved in matters well beyond the purely military. Though I did the best I could in each piece of writing, driven as I was by pride and fear, I suppose it was the sheer bulk and the regularity of writing that helped me most.

When I got out of the Army, I think I wrote better. I know I wrote faster.

My Army experience convinces me that students of writing should be urged, or required, to write more and to write more often. But that, you will say, would put an unbearable burden on the teacher who has to correct and grade all that writing. I have a solution. I also have a confession to make. Toward the end of my first year of teaching, worn down by those four sections of Freshman English, I found a way to give my students more writing practice and yet spare myself. I have never confessed this until now. I hope the statute of limitations has run out and I cannot be made to return part of my salary.

What I did was to require my students to write two themes a week instead of the usual one theme. Did that mean I had to correct 240 themes a week (two times 120 students), and did it drive me nuts? No, and not just because many must have thought me nuts already. You see, I read only half as many papers per week as I had been reading, 60 instead of 120. Do you wonder how I managed it? I shall tell you, although I never told the Chairman of the Department.

After each two-week period, with four themes written, I brought to class four carefully folded slips of paper. Each had a number on it, from one to four. I put the slips of paper into a hat, and then asked one of the students to come forward, stir the slips of paper, and select one. If, say, the number three was chosen, I read theme three, and only theme three. The grade on that theme was the grade for the two weeks. If a student wished to take a chance and skip one theme, and it turned out to be number three, the student received an "F" for the two weeks. There was very little skipping, I assure you.

Since I read only half as many themes as before, though the students wrote twice as many, I read each paper more carefully and wrote more extensive comments. Probably most of what I had to say applied pretty well to the three unread papers, or at least I hope so. As for the students, they got twice as much writing practice as the students in other instructors' sections. You may wonder that they didn't squeal on me. I think it was the thrill of gambling that caused them to play along. Anyhow, I did this only in the last weeks of the year, and I was leaving (voluntarily) to take another job. . . .

Years later, many years later, I had a letter from one of the students in my Freshman English. He had become the president of a university. He remembered my "lottery," as he called it, and said he still possessed some of the papers on which I had written comments. He did not say, but I like to think he became a university president because of his ability to write with such clarity and effectiveness.

Now that you know everything you have always wanted to know but have been afraid to ask about writing, how about literature?

III
English Survey

The first literature course I was considered competent to teach was Survey of English Literature. It was also known as Sophomore Survey, though it was not sophomores who were being surveyed, except by young instructors such as I. That was before I was married, when I was still looking over the girls in my classes, and imagining. To be truthful, this is something I continued to do even after I was married.

The reason I was considered competent to teach the Survey, after apprenticeship as a teacher of Freshman English, was that no great depth of learning was required. The descriptive title of the course was "From *Beowulf* to Hardy," and the important thing was to get to Hardy on or before the last class meeting. I understand the Survey now gets to T. S. Eliot, which indicates either that students read faster or that they know less about more. Anyhow, if they are taking the course for Pass-Fail, there is no need to pick up all the fine points necessary to make an A or B.

The most useful item in teaching the Survey is a syllabus or, if it were more accurately named, a timetable. This shows, for instance, where you should be by November 6 and how many days or minutes can be given to Milton. I always enjoyed teaching the Survey, because I sometimes got behind on purpose and then hurried over writers I didn't like or didn't know much about.

The main thing, I learned, was to hurry but not to seem hurried. I taught the Survey for many years, even when I did not have to, and became fairly good at it. Many times I concluded a lecture precisely as the bell rang, as if putting an audible period to my final sentence. For the teacher of the Survey, this is the ultimate achievement, bringing a flush of pride to the cheeks. When this happened I felt like a virtuoso pianist as he triumphantly struck the last notes of a sonata. Like the pianist, I deserved cries of "Bravo!" and a standing ovation, but had to be satisfied with the slamming shut of notebooks and such stretchings and yawnings as follow fifty minutes of captivity.

The key word in teaching the Survey is "cover," which is very different from uncover or discover. To cover means that the name of the author must be mentioned and, if there is time, his birth and death dates. Since I could hardly wait to get to Shakespeare, I made something of a sacrifice when I dwelt long enough on Spenser to point out that his name is spelled with an "s" instead of a "c." But I know my students appreciated it. They might forget the rhyme scheme of the Spenserian stanza, or who Gloriana was, but that spelling would, I hoped, stick with them for life.

Those who are taking or teaching the Survey may get momentary relief by reading these excerpts from my *English Lit Relit*. What I have done in these passages, chosen with great difficulty, is to make a survey of a survey.

BEOWULF

The author is unknown, and this has led to several interesting theories. One is that the author kept his name secret, after he realized what he had written, for the sake of his family. Another is that there was not a single author but many authors, which would account for the length of the poem. Still another theory is that there was no author, and the whole thing was a hoax, dreamed up by English professors who had to have something with which to begin the Survey course.

The poem is considered an epic because of its long speeches, its digressions, its repetition, its bloodshed, and its being required.

Beowulf was a noble hero. After tearing off Grendel's arm, instead of keeping it as a souvenir he generously hung it over the doorway to Hrothgar's hall so that all might enjoy it. Later he also gave Grendel's head to Hrothgar, apparently knowing Hrothgar liked that sort of thing. Fortunately Beowulf finally went back to his homeland, else Hrothgar's hall, Heorot, would have been full of bits and pieces.[1]

GEOFFREY CHAUCER

Despite his trouble with spelling, Chaucer was the greatest writer of the fourteenth century. At one time he was controller of customs in London, customs apparently having got out of control. But he got his best material for writing when the King appointed him inspector of the sewers along the Thames. What he reported to the King is not known, but he saw some things that had to wait more than five centuries to be written about.

Chaucer left many of his poems unfinished. Something may have come up, such as his suddenly remembering an appointment with the doctor for his Black Death inocula-

---

[1] The poem has what is called "grim Anglo-Saxon humor." Warriors held their sides—not because of laughter but because of sword thrusts.

tions, and when he got back to his desk he wasn't in the mood.

Some of the tales in *The Canterbury Tales* are so rough, bawdy, and low class that they have universal appeal.

SIR PHILIP SIDNEY

Those who think the sonnet cycle, which Sidney invented, was a means of transportation, will be disappointed to learn that his was a series of 108 sonnets, written to another man's wife.[1]

Sidney died heroically at the battle of Zutphen, declining a cup of water and letting another soldier have it. This has been praised for centuries as an act of chivalry, though there are some who think Sidney wasn't thirsty.

SIR WALTER RALEIGH

Raleigh was in and out of favor with the Queen. When he was out of favor he was in the Tower and when he was in favor he was out of the Tower.

He was imprisoned for thirteen years by James I. This gave him ample leisure to write. "What can I write that will take me thirteen years?" he asked himself. Very wisely he chose to write a *History of the World*. This was better than keeping track of the years by making marks on the wall.

EDMUND SPENCER

One of Spenser's early works was his *Shepherd's Calendar*. Fortunately, time meant little to shepherds, because they could never have figured out the day of the week

---

[1] A less plausible theory, in view of their passionate nature, is that they were addressed to his own wife.

from it. Colin Clout and his friends stayed out of doors day after day, rain or shine, and gradually became rustic.

Spenser's greatest work was *The Faerie Queene*. It is one of the longest poems in English, and anyone who says he has read every word of it is not to be trusted.

WILLIAM SHAKESPEARE

The greatest of the Elizabethan writers was William Shakespeare. What made him so great was that he managed to get Bacon, Marlowe, and the Earl of Oxford to write his plays for him.

Shakespeare's plays are divided into three types: histories, tragedies, and comedies. Some critics add two other kinds: good and bad. The tragedies end with the principal characters stabbed or poisoned. The histories end with the principal characters killed or crowned. The comedies, which often have a tragic element, end with the principal characters married.

In addition to his plays Shakespeare wrote two narrative poems and CLIV sonnets.

BEN JONSON

Jonson was a strong, burly bricklayer, quick to anger. "Twice he killed a man in a single combat," writes his biographer, not explaining why Jonson thought it necessary to kill the poor fellow more than once. He must have been angry indeed.

Many of Ben Jonson's plays are based on the idea that people are composed of four humors: blood, phlegm, bile, and black bile. According to Jonson's theory a person with too much phlegm would be phlegmatic, though the doctor would probably call it a hard cold and prescribe two aspirin.

Over Jonson's grave in Westminster Abbey is the inscription "O rare Ben Jonson." What was so unusual about Ben was that he was buried vertically, to save space. His position in Westminster, as well as in English literature, is secure.

FRANCIS BACON

Bacon held many jobs under Queen Elizabeth, and at one time was Lord Keeper. Keeping lords, however, was no easy job, a kept lord making even more demands than a kept woman.

Bacon's best-known writings are his *Essays*. They are loved for many reasons, such as their being so short. The title of each of the fifty-eight essays begins with "Of," which gives unity to the collection. The essays are full of common sense and good advice, as in "Of Expense," when Bacon says, "Riches are for spending." Or in "Of Building," when he sagely remarks, "Houses are built to live in." This came to him in a moment of inspiration, and the more you think of it the better it seems than, say, "Houses are built to pay taxes on."

ELIZABETHAN LYRICS

England was known at this time as "a nation of singing birds." Everyone was a-twitter. For instance there was the rather naughty song, "Back and side go bare, go bare."[1] For joy and conviviality consider Samuel Daniel's "Love is a sickness full of woes" and John Fletcher's "Lay a garland on my hearse."[2] However the lyrics of this period can be summed up with the delightful refrain from Thomas Nash's "Spring":

---

[1] Nothing, however, is said about the front.
[2] See also Thomas Campion's "There is a garden in her face." People grew flowers and vegetables in the most unlikely places in those days.

Cuckoo, jug-jug, pu-we, to-witta-woo!

SEVENTEENTH-CENTURY POETRY

Writers of the seventeenth century fall into two groups, the Cavaliers or Roundheads and the Puritans or Square-heads. The Cavaliers believed in having a good time now, in case now is all there is. The Puritans believed in waiting for the Hereafter, which would last longer. Middle-of-the-roaders had a good time all week, but went to church on Sunday.

JOHN DONNE

John Donne is hard to classify. In fact he is often hard to understand. Dr. Johnson called him "metaphysical," which seems as good a term as any, especially when you learn that metaphysical means "of or pertaining to metaphysics."

Among his poems is one in which he tells the reader to "Go and catch a falling star," "Get with child a mandrake root," and do other things that most would find difficult. The critic was right who said, "Donne makes demands on his readers."[1]

Donne posed in his shroud for the monument to be placed over his tomb. He wanted people to know how he looked without having to peer inside.

ROBERT HERRICK

In his *Hesperides,* Herrick explains how roses, that at first were white, became red. It seems that they blushed

---

[1] Donne could also be pretty irritable, as when he said, "For God's sake hold your tongue and let me love." Apparently someone had walked in and started chattering when Donne was busy.

upon discovering that the breasts of Sapho, one of Herrick's girl friends, were even whiter.[1]

Another interesting thing about Herrick is that he trained a pet pig to drink from a tankard. "Watch me," he kept saying, until finally the pig got the idea.

OTHER LYRISTS

George Wither was aptly named because of his "Shall I, wasting in despair?" He wasted slowly, however, living until he was almost eighty, a dried-up little old man. And there was Henry Vaughan, who once remarked, in a casual, offhand manner, "I saw Eternity the other night." Anyone else would have been more excited, phoning the police or calling a press conference. There was also Thomas Carew, who finally grew tired of being asked stupid questions, such as what does Jove do with faded roses and where do falling stars wind up and where does the Phoenix build its nest. "Ask me no more," he said, and there was a wild look in his eyes.

Sir John Suckling is remembered for his

> Out upon it, I have loved
> Three whole days together!
> And am like to love three more,
> If it prove fair weather.

It is not clear why he couldn't have kept going just as well or better if it rained, unless he did his loving outdoors.

Richard Lovelace wrote those famous lines:

> Stone walls do not a prison make,
> Nor iron bars a cage.

---

[1] Botanists scoff at this explanation. But then, they never saw Sapho as Herrick did.

Jailed for political offenses, he spent enough time in prison, beating on the walls and tugging at the bars, to know better.[1]

JOHN MILTON

Milton was known at Cambridge as "the lady of Christ's," which was a somewhat misleading nickname, since he later married three times.[2] He also believed in the divine right of kings to be executed.

Lycidas is a pastoral elegy about the death of a college friend, Edward King. Milton and his friend were very close. "For we were nursed upon the self-same hill," Milton says, the two mothers apparently sitting there with their infants, looking down into the valley and chatting the while.

Milton's purpose in writing *Paradise Lost* was to justify the ways of God to men, even he being unable to write a poem long enough to justify the ways of men to God or of men to men. The Miltonic style is apparent in the opening sentence. It runs for sixteen lines before the poet can find a way to turn it off.[3] After eating the Forbidden Fruit, Adam and Eve notice, to their embarrassment, that they are stark naked. Though they put on some fig leaves, they are unable, as Milton says, to hide their guilt.

When Milton said he was writing a sequel to *Paradise Lost,* readers eagerly looked forward to something on the order of *Satan Rides Again* or *Return of the Serpent. Paradise Regained* wasn't quite what they had expected.

---

[1] Or perhaps he had gone stir crazy. His fellow prisoners shook their heads. *They* knew what was keeping them in.

[2] Better than average for a Puritan.

[3] The poem is full of apostrophes, but what it needs is periods.

SEVENTEENTH-CENTURY PROSE

Many of the prose writers of this period were clergymen, supported by the church or the government, and there was no need for them to write anything good enough to sell.

ROBERT BURTON

Robert Burton is said to have written *The Anatomy of Melancholy* to keep himself from going insane. "His mind was dark," says his biographer, having looked inside, probably through an ear, and been unable to see a thing.

Burton had another way of cheering himself up, besides reading and writing about melancholy. This was listening to bargemen swear. When he left them, with their curses ringing in his ears, he somehow felt better.

SIR THOMAS BROWNE

Unlike Burton, a clergyman who wrote about medicine, Sir Thomas Browne was a doctor who wrote about religion. His great work was *Religio Medici,* widely thought (by those who have not read it) to be about Religio, a relative of Lorenzo.

It is a good idea to keep an unabridged dictionary at hand while reading Sir Thomas Browne, unless you commonly use such words as indigitate, piaculous, ubiquitary, tapid, and transpeciate.

IZAAK WALTON

Izaak Walton is best known for *The Compleat Angler* (often misspelled *The Complete Angler*). This work takes the form of a discussion by an angler, a hunter, and a falconer during a fishing expedition. The three men talk steadily for five days, arguing, quoting poems, and frightening away the fish. Walton professes to like a quiet life, but only if he has no one to listen to him tell how to put a hook through a lob-worm or how to dress a chub.[1]

JOHN BUNYAN

The title of Bunyan's *Pilgrim's Progress* confuses many persons who think that, with all that walking, it should be *Pilgrim's Bunyan*. Bunyan wrote *Pilgrim's Progress* when he was in prison, serving a twelve-year term for preaching. Surely his sermons couldn't have been *that* bad.

SAMUEL PEPYS

In his *Diary,* Pepys tells all. He dwells on such intimate matters as sending his mother some tainted cheese, worrying over the fact that his wife's hair is falling out, and singing hymns in the morning before getting out of bed. It was for getting into bed, however, that he is best known. The most famous quotation from Pepys, who was something of an old roué, is "And so to bed."

THE RESTORATION

The Restoration was not quite so spectacular as may at first be supposed. Charles I was not restored, or even revived. Charles II assumed the throne, bringing from France a large supply of snuff, perfumed handkerchiefs, fans, courtiers, and courtesans. The Puritans had kept the theaters closed, thinking them a hotbed of immorality.[2] With the Restoration, everything was out in the open, especially with actresses wearing low-cut dresses and being corseted in the middle. Wycherley's *Country Wife* was

---

[1] Until it is caught, the chub goes around undressed. It finds it easier to swim that way.
[2] The very word "hotbed" made them blush.

widely hailed by the critics as "coarse," "indecent," and "lecherous," and the theater was jammed.

JOHN DRYDEN

According to one literary historian, "Dryden's dates are very suggestive to the student of English literature." They are 1631–1700, and what is so suggestive about them is hard to see.[1]

Dryden's plays were mostly tragedies, but he went on writing, undismayed. He also wrote a satire, *Absolom and Achitophel,* about Absolom (Monmouth), Achitophel (Shaftesbury), David (Charles II), and others (others).

EIGHTEENTH-CENTURY LITERATURE

The most interesting thing about eighteenth-century literature is that, impatient to get started, it began in 1688. Most works were set in London and emphasized cheating, thievery, blackmail, and whoring. Commonplace though these themes were, they were handled with wit.[2]

DEFOE

Defoe is said to have had a "genius for lying like truth." For instance in *A Journal of the Plague Year* he writes about the plague of 1665 as if he had been a grown man then, rather than a five-year-old boy. But instead of saying, "It's a lie," critics said, "What realism!" He continued lying in *Robinson Crusoe, Moll Flanders,* and other works and made such a success of it that other writers took it up. However they changed the name of it from lying to fic-

---

[1] Compare, for instance, 1631–1700 with 38–23–36.

[2] Many have tried to define wit, but no one has surpassed Dr. Johnson's famous definition, to wit: "Wit is wit."

tion. Somehow, prose fiction sounds better than prose lying.

JONATHAN SWIFT

One of Swift's early works was *A Tale of a Tub.* It shows the genius of Swift by not being about a tub. In *A Modest Proposal* Swift suggests that babies of the poor people of Ireland be fattened until they are a year old and then sold for meat. Why Swift's proposal was not snapped up is hard to understand. It is not only a practical solution of the population problem but full of mouth-watering recipes.

With regard to *Gulliver's Travels,* some feel that in referring to human beings as "the most pernicious race of little odious vermin that Nature ever suffered to crawl upon the face of the earth," Swift was overdoing it a little. But you can't please everyone.

ADDISON AND STEELE

Addison and Steele were forerunners of such literary partnerships as Gilbert and Sullivan and prove that two heads are almost as good as one good one. They were joint editors of the *Tatler* and *Spectator,* which could be compared to modern newspapers except for their basic aim, which was to popularize morality and culture.

ALEXANDER POPE

Pope was only four feet six inches tall, which may be why some critics have never been able to see him as a poet. As a boy, Pope seems to have been mathematically inclined. "I lisped in numbers, for the numbers came," he tells us in his *Epistle to Dr. Arbuthnot,* and we can hear the lad counting, "thixth, theven," and tho on. In *An Essay on Criticism* Pope sets down the rules for good writing. "A little learning is a dangerous thing," he says at one point, warning writers to think twice before fooling around with education.[1]

The Rape of the Lock isn't as pornographic as the title would suggest.[2]

SAMUEL RICHARDSON

It was not until he was fifty that Richardson published his first novel, *Pamela, or Virtue Rewarded*. It took four volumes for virtue to triumph.

Richardson's greatest success was *Clarissa Harlowe*. Clarissa is drugged and raped by her dissolute lover, Robert Lovelace, who is stabbed in the end.[3] The novel is written in the form of letters from one character to another, and considering how busy everyone is with chases, imprisonments, escapes, and whatnot, it is a wonder anyone has time to sign his name or seal an envelope.

HENRY FIELDING

Fielding is best remembered for *Tom Jones*. At the beginning of the novel Squire Allworthy finds a baby in his bed. Since the Squire is single, and it is a single bed, something is obviously amiss. It turns out that the baby is Tom Jones, a foundling. He is a pretty baby, and the Squire and his sister Bridget are always foundling him. The most important thing about *Tom Jones* is the characters. As one critic says, "The huge canvas, when filled, contains forty figures." If you can visualize a huge canvas

---

[1] Brain surgeons will appreciate Pope's "Most have the seeds of judgment in their mind." So that's what they are, they muse, poking around with tweezers.
[2] It was not Pope but another poet who said, "The Muse and I have been cohabiting, and we have had couplets."
[3] He made the mistake of turning his back.

bag stuffed with people, you will get some idea of Fielding's accomplishment.

LAURENCE STERNE

Though Sterne was a country parson, he was a cut-up and practical joker. "In full middle life," says his biographer, "he pulled off his wig and donned the cap and bells of Yorick." It must have been a startling scene, the way he yanked off that wig and grabbed Yorick's cap and bells. His wife went insane.[1]

Sterne had finished two volumes of *Tristram Shandy* and was trying it on some guests when several of them drowsed off. In a rage he threw the manuscript into the fire, but someone rescued it. By that time everyone was awake.

The end of *Tristram Shandy* comes not when Sterne has finished his story but when he has run out of dashes and asterisks.

THE GRAVEYARD SCHOOL

The poets of the Graveyard School sat around happily in cemeteries, reading the inscriptions on tombstones, envying the dead, and hoping to see a ghost. A newly opened grave was always a thrill, good for twenty or thirty lines of speculation about skulls, coffins, and worms. Here is a typical passage from Robert Blair's *The Grave:*

Doors creak, and windows clap, and night's foul
bird,
Rooked in the spire, screams loud.

---

[1] "Sterne's ways were unpredictable," says one writer, "and his household was a constant jangle." The jangle, of course, came from the bells on his cap.

The windows seem to have shared Blair's enthusiasm, clapping that way. As for the poor bird, no wonder it screamed, the spire having rooked it.[1]

THOMAS GRAY

Gray was subject to fits of depression, during one of which he wrote his *Elegy Written in a Country Churchyard*. A careful craftsman, he worked over the poem for seven years, which figures out to almost exactly three weeks to a line.

The central theme of the poem seems to be that "The paths of glory lead but to the grave." In other words, everybody eventually dies. The thought is not original with Gray.

THE AGE OF JOHNSON

The Age of Johnson was greater than the Age of Pope, Johnson living to seventy-five and Pope to fifty-six.

SAMUEL JOHNSON

For many years Johnson was very poor. This gave him his chief motive for writing: money. One difference between Johnson and most writers is that he not only wrote for money but admitted it. "No one but a blockhead ever wrote except for money," he declared, and no one ever dared call Dr. Johnson a blockhead to his face.

Johnson hated Americans, Scots, Irish, French, Italians, and Whigs. "He was a good hater," says one of his biographers admiringly. But he liked cats, which kept him from a perfect record. With publication of his *Dictionary*, he became known as the Great Lexicographer. Those who

---

[1] Perhaps the bird lit on the tip, which was sharper than it had suspected.

don't know the meaning of lexicographer can look it up in Johnson's *Dictionary*.[1]

In his later years Johnson received a pension and was able to write less and talk more. It is interesting to conjecture about Johnson's literary career had he been paid for talking and not for writing, instead of the other way around.

JAMES BOSWELL

Boswell is described as having "a burning, steady eye." It must have been disconcerting to people the first time they saw him. He is also said to have had an eye for the ladies, though whether this was the burning one or the other one is not made clear.

A book that would make racier reading than Boswell's *Life of Johnson* would be Johnson's *Life of Boswell*.

OLIVER GOLDSMITH

In *The Deserted Village* Goldsmith yearns for the Good Old Days of simple living. Goldsmith was writing in 1770, and knew nothing of freeways, parking problems, smog, and the population explosion.[2]

Goldsmith studied medicine for a time but never practiced. Lacking patients, he once prescribed something for himself, when he was very ill. The remedy aggravated the malady and Goldsmith died.[3]

THE PRE-ROMANTICS

Cowper had attacks of insanity, Macpherson was a forger, Burns drank too much, Blake had weird visions,

---

[1] Johnson defines a lexicographer as "A writer of dictionaries, a harmless drudge," and he ought to know.
[2] In *The Deserted Village* he worries about underpopulation.
[3] Had he lingered on, he could have sued himself for malpractice.

and Chatterton committed suicide. These are the Pre-Romantics, preparing us for the incest, wife desertion, and drug addiction of the Great Romantics.

ROBERT BURNS

Robert Burns is admired in Scotland for having worked his way up from poverty in the country to poverty in the city. As a boy on his father's farm he read poetry while ploughing, and it is no wonder he had some of the crookedest furrows in Ayrshire.

Many of Burns's poems have to do with his heart, which gave him a good deal of trouble. For instance there is "My heart is a-breaking, dear tittie,"[1] and his famous

> My heart's in the Highlands, my heart is not
> here;
> My heart's in the Highlands, a-chasing the deer.

Burns, who was then in the Lowlands, must have had difficulty keeping up his blood pressure. But that is nothing compared with how terrified the deer must have been if it looked back over its shoulder.

WILLIAM BLAKE

Blake's poems in his *Songs of Innocence* are easy enough to comprehend. For instance there are his lines to a sick rose, beginning, "O Rose, thou art sick!" The rose is in a bad way, and should be transplanted from the flower bed to its deathbed. Sometimes, to be absolutely sure his meaning is clear, Blake repeats a difficult line, as in

---

[1] Whatever you think, "tittie" means "sister."

Little Lamb, I'll tell thee,
Little Lamb, I'll tell thee.

But the reader may be a little uncertain about the meaning of poems such as *Jerusalem* and *The Book of Thel.* If so, he will be grateful to the critic who explains these works by calling them "roseate and cerulean fancies on a gossamer texture woven out of the songs of Shakespeare and the echoes of Fingal's airy hall."

THE ROMANTIC PERIOD

At this time the noble savage was greatly admired, and many people went to remote places to seek him out and get his opinions on current social and political problems. Some travelers failed to return, having run into ignoble savages by mistake.

WILLIAM WORDSWORTH

The greatest of the Romantic poets was William Wordsworth. His greatness is indicated by his ability to write, in *The Prelude*, nearly 8000 lines about the growth of his mind.[1]

As he tells us in the Preface to the *Lyrical Ballads*, he believed in using "language really used by men." He therefore listened intently to idiot boys, beggars, and old leech gatherers. This accounts for such powerful, manly lines as "And then an open field they crossed" and "Right glad was he when he beheld her."

He had a way of talking to daisies ("Daisy! again I talk to thee"), and people who saw him down on his knees, in

---

[1] At that, it was just the beginning of a much longer poem he was unable to finish, since he lived to be only eighty.

an animated conversation, tapped their heads or pretended not to notice.[1]

SAMUEL TAYLOR COLERIDGE

"Coleridge wrote only when the Muse called him," writes his biographer. That explains why his best writing was done before he was thirty, since his hearing declined as he grew older. Then too, he was always stopping work for an opium break.

The Rime of the Ancient Mariner is about an old mariner who stops a wedding guest to tell him his strange story. Meanwhile the bride, who is waiting for all the guests to arrive, is about to explode. "Red as a rose is she," Coleridge says. The Ancient Mariner's story has an important moral: Never shoot an albatross that is harmlessly hanging around. The next thing you know it will be hanging around your neck.

Christabel is Coleridge's most medieval poem. Notice the medievalism of such a line as

Tu———whit!———Tu———whoo!

SIR WALTER SCOTT

Scott loved anything old. He built his home, Abbotsford, in the style of a medieval castle. He also loved the supernatural, and was delighted when the house grew old enough for the doors to squeak. On windy, rainy nights he would lie in bed and listen to the ghosts of Scottish heroes as they wafted around in their ectoplasm.[2]

---

[1] It was embarrassing to be introduced to a flower that just kept nodding.
[2] Anyone who wishes to know a little more about Scott can read the seven-volume biography by Lockhart, his son-in-law.

CHARLES LAMB

Charles Lamb was apparently a sickly youth, since he went to school at Christ's Hospital. Later he was put away for a while in a madhouse. He was not really insane, but people got the idea he was from some of his puns.[1]

One of Lamb's essays is *A Dissertation Upon Roast Pig*, explaining how to roast a pig and burn down your house at the same time. The main thing is to lock all the doors so the pig can't get out. As Lamb says, in his simple, informal way, "Of all the delicacies in the whole *mundus edibilis*, I will maintain it to be the most delicate—*princeps obsoniorum.*"

WILLIAM HAZLITT

One of Lamb's circle was William Hazlitt, but unlike Lamb, who had mostly friends, Hazlitt had mostly enemies. "He stood alone," it has been said, unless he had had a little too much to drink. In *My First Acquaintance with Poets*, about his meeting with Coleridge, he begins: "My father was a Dissenting Minister at W—m in Shropshire." Most writers would have told the name of the town, which was Wem, but Hazlitt held back. People thought it must surely be a vowel he left out, as in "d—mn," and guessed Wam, Wim, Wom, and Wum before they got it right.

THOMAS DE QUINCEY

Like Coleridge, De Quincey became addicted to opium. As the title of *Confessions of an English Opium Eater* indicates, it was English opium he ate, since he was unable to afford the imported variety.

Despite the opium habit and his preoccupation with

---

[1] The author of the present volume has himself been getting some curious looks.

sudden death,[1] De Quincey lived to be seventy-four. This may be attributed to his habit of deep breathing, described in *Sighs from the Depths*.

GEORGE GORDON, LORD BYRON

Byron blamed his ancestry when he got out of line a little. "I can't help it," he said, after a night of debauchery. By having a daughter by his half-sister, Augusta, he hoped to confuse the genealogists. The last eight years of his life Byron spent as an exile, traveling about from woman to woman.

In *Childe Harold's Pilgrimage*, Childe Harold is no childe, or at any rate he is old enough to have run through Sin's long labyrinth, which must have taken a little time, even at high speed. Byron has trouble keeping track of his hero. "But where is Harold?" he asks at one point. If Byron doesn't know, how can he expect the reader to?

PERCY BYSSHE SHELLEY

Shelley was such a firm believer in freedom, justice, equality, and the brotherhood of man that he was thought unbalanced. In school he was known as "Mad Shelley."

He was, we are told, "always yearning for the unattainable." An example of this is in his *Ode to the West Wind*, when he wishes he were a dead leaf. This seems a modest enough ambition, but Shelley never made it.

Everything, to Shelley, was like something else, and he could never quite make up his mind what. Thus in *To a Skylark* a skylark is like a cloud of fire, like an unbodied joy,[2] like a star, like a poet, like a high-born maiden, like a

---

[1] See his *The Vision of Sudden Death* and *Dream Fugue on the Theme of Sudden Death*. It is a pity De Quincey lived before the era of the motor car.

[2] This may be a little hard for you to picture.

glowworm, and like a rose. Without the word "like," Shelley would have been helpless.

JOHN KEATS

Keats loved everything Greek. An example is the Elgin marbles, which he could imagine boys playing with in ancient Athens. One of his most Greek works is *Endymion*.[1] It contains such lines as

> And now, as deep into the woods as we
> Might mark a lynx's eye.

How to get a lynx to stand still long enough for you to mark its eye is something Keats does not explain.

One of Endymion's difficulties, as a lover, is that he is always going to sleep. His dreams, however, are almost as good as the real thing.[2] In many of his poems Keats is preoccupied with sleep. He was lucky not to have gone sleepless for three thousand years, like Prometheus. In his *Ode to a Nightingale* Keats becomes a bit confused. "Do I wake or sleep?" he says. You sympathize with him and his need to know.

We shall conclude our treatment of Keats with those oft-quoted lines from his *Ode to a Grecian Urn:*

> Heard melodies are sweet, but those unheard
> Are sweeter.

As well as we can figure it out, Keats means it is nice to listen to music but nicer not to.

---

[1] "It's Greek to me," students have said for years.
[2] Describing one of Endymion's dreams of kissing, Keats refers to "Those lips, O slippery blisses." Endymion seems to have had trouble getting traction.

THE VICTORIAN ERA

According to one historian, "The period of sentiment and self-indulgence ended when Victoria came to the throne. The English people became high-minded, modest, self-righteous, and enterprising." What kept them from doing anything wrong was their being afraid Queen Victoria might make some such devastating remark as "We are not amused."

THOMAS CARLYLE

Thomas Carlyle's belief in hard work is perhaps traceable to his birthplace, Ecclefechan, which is about as hard to spell and pronounce as the birthplace of any English author.[1] He had a Scotch burr, probably picked up while walking through the fields. With this burr and a bad case of stomach trouble, it is no wonder he was crotchety and irritable.

Probably no English writer has relied so heavily on the comma. A typical sentence in *Sartor Resartus* begins: "To such readers as have reflected, what can be called reflecting, on man's life, and happily discovered, in contradiction to my Profit-and-Loss Philosophy, speculative and practical, that. . . ." Some say that after his wife died Carlyle was in a comma the rest of his life.

ALFRED, LORD TENNYSON

One of Tennyson's best-known poems is *Locksley Hall,* especially the line, "In the spring a young man's fancy lightly turns to thoughts of love."[2] For some reason, this

---

[1] Being born in Ecclefechan he couldn't help, but Craigenputtock, where he later lived, was his own choice.
[2] Another version of this is "In the spring a young man's fancy, but a young woman's fancier."

line is better known than the line rhyming with it, "In the spring a livelier iris changes on the burnished dove." As for Tennyson's *Idylls of the King*,[1] some critics feel that King Arthur resembles Queen Victoria's husband, Prince Albert. If so, this did not stand in the way of Tennyson's appointment as Poet Laureate.

THE BROWNINGS

In her *Sonnets from the Portuguese* Elizabeth counted (and recounted) all the ways she loved Robert. Robert called them "the finest sonnets written in any language since Shakespeare's." Actually he thought them better than Shakespeare's, but tried not to be prejudiced because they were by his wife and about him.

Some of Browning's lines are puzzling. In *Andrea del Sarto* he maintains that "A man's reach should exceed his grasp," which is something you should try sometime, but not out where people can see you. And then there is his "Grow old along with me," which is almost impossible if you were born after 1889, the year Browning died.

Browning had good health and enormous vitality. His only surgery was when he had "Italy" engraved on his heart. The ordinary person would have been satisfied to have had it tattoed on his arm.

CHARLES DICKENS

Charles Dickens was fortunate in having an unhappy childhood and a father who spent a good deal of time in debtors' prison. Otherwise he would not have had the material for such novels as *Oliver Twist, David Copperfield, Bleak House,* and *Hard Times.* He roamed the streets of London looking for people with odd names, a telephone book not yet being available. Consider Squeers,

---

[1] Actually the King was a busy man, far from idyll.

Bumble, Quilp, Scrooge, Smike, Heep, Gamp, Swiveller, Jellyby, and Gride.

"London," says one critic, "was Dickens' laboratory—the people, the food, the drink, the very smells." But if Dickens stood on the street corner sniffing, his readers are usually sniffling. "He tugs at the heartstrings," we are told, and the heartstrings seem to be attached to the tear ducts and whatever it is that makes a lump in the throat.

WILLIAM MAKEPEACE THACKERAY

Thackeray's *Vanity Fair* is an unusual novel in that it has no hero. The author makes up for this, however, by having two heroines, Becky Sharp and Amelia Sedley. Becky has a better time of it, since she is richly endowed with the qualities most useful in getting ahead in the world: ambition, unscrupulousness, and immorality.[1]

"Many attempts have been made to compare Thackeray and Dickens as novelists," says one critic, "but the two authors are so different that this would be as much to the purpose as to compare chalk with cheese." What this critic does not say is which author is which.

THE BRONTËS

The father of the Brontë sisters was perpetual curate of Haworth, which means that he could have kept the job forever if he hadn't had the bad luck to die. The rectory in which Charlotte, Emily, and Anne lived was not exactly a fun place. Their father was a tyrant. Their mother and two sisters died of tuberculosis. Their brother Branwell was a confirmed drunkard.[2] But the three sisters livened things

---

[1] Becky is not only sharp but hard.
[2] Confirmed by friends, relatives, and pub owners.

up by writing stories and poems which they read aloud in the evenings, trying to drown out the mournful sound of the wind in the moors.

Charlotte's *Jane Eyre* and Emily's *Wuthering Heights* are said to have given Victorian readers their first taste of romance and passion.[1]

One of the virtues of *Jane Eyre* is the realistic dialogue, as when Jane exclaims: "The human and fallible should not arrogate a power with which the divine and perfect alone can be safely entrusted." In *Wuthering Heights* the villain, Heathcliff, dies in the last chapter with a sneer on his face. It was there for good, though everything else about Heathcliff was bad.

GEORGE ELIOT

George Eliot was born Mary Ann Evans, and those who saw her, with her square jaw and enormous head, agree that she did the right thing in changing her name from Mary to George. It was while she was living in sin with George Henry Lewes that George Eliot wrote *Silas Marner*, a highly moral novel. Lewes is said to have "discovered and roused her creative gift," perhaps one time when he was just fiddling around.[2]

Bulwer-Lytton said he thought the defects of *Adam Bede* were the use of dialect and the marriage of Adam. "I would have my teeth drawn," George Eliot said, "rather than give up either."[3] She was a very determined woman.

---

[1] They smacked their lips, but not loud enough for anyone to hear.
[2] Though not married, they lived as man and wife. "Bring me my slippers, George," one George would say. "Yes, George," the other George would reply.
[3] Whether she meant having her teeth pulled or having a picture drawn of them is not clear. The latter might have been more of a sacrifice.

THE PRE-RAPHAELITES

To the Pre-Raphaelites, the Middle Ages were the Good Old Days, with their plagues, tyranny, superstition, and religious persecution. The Brotherhood felt cheated by the substitution of the materialism and ugliness of the machine age.

DANTE GABRIEL ROSSETTI

Rossetti's favorite theme was love, and he found his ideal image of womanhood in Elizabeth Siddal, a clerk in a milliner's shop. She looked so good modeling hats that he got her to pose for him without a hat, or anything.[1] Then, satisfied that he knew what he was getting, he married her. Two years after their marriage, Elizabeth died. Rossetti was so distraught that he buried the manuscript of a new book of poems with her. However seven years later, after thinking it over, he had the poems exhumed and published them. After all, Elizabeth couldn't read them, down there in that poor light.

The Blessed Damozel tells of a damozel who is leaning over a bar in Heaven.[2] Her robe is all unfastened in front and, as Rossetti says, she has leaned there

> Until her bosom must have made
> The bar she leaned on warm.

That is the poet for you. Looked at in another way, it must have made her bosom cold.

CHRISTINA ROSSETTI

Christina Rossetti was Dante's sister.[3] She was the only woman in the Pre-Raphaelite Brotherhood, and must have

---

[1] Since Rossetti was not only a poet but a painter, this was quite all right.
[2] Some will find it hard to believe there is a bar in the place, or a bartender.
[3] Dante Rossetti's, that is.

felt a little out of place. *Goblin Market* is Christina's most famous poem. She originally called it *A Peep at the Goblins,* but her brother Dante, annoyed at her constant yapping about death, may have said, "Not another peep out of you."[1]

WILLIAM MORRIS

William Morris is probably the only English poet to have a chair named after him.[2] He often went to factories, where he lectured workers about the joy of work, and they quit work to stand around and listen.

In *The Defence of Guenevere,* Guenevere confesses that she and Launcelot kissed, but swears that was all they did. Her description of that innocent kiss shows how people did such things in those days:

> When both our mouths went wandering in one
> way,
> And aching sorely, met among the leaves;
> Our hands being left behind strained far away.

We can imagine Guenevere exclaiming happily, "Look, Launcelot, no hands!" In fact both of the lovers left their hands far behind, perhaps in a pile of leaves, being too busy with their lips to notice.

ALGERNON CHARLES SWINBURNE

Swinburne wrote some great lines. Among those that linger in one's mind are:

---

[1] In *Looking Forward* she eagerly looks forward to dying, being buried, and having plants grow out of her. "Barren through life, but in death bearing fruit" is the way she expresses this interesting idea of having flowers and berries for offspring.

[2] Other than an endowed professorship at a university.

I shall never be friends again with roses.[1]
Villon, our sad bad glad mad[2] brother's name.[3]
I am sick of singing.[4]

CONCLUSION

Though it had suffered a severe blow, English literature
continued after the Pre-Raphaelites. Thomas Hardy, for
instance, wrote novels in which he somehow managed to
make everything come out for the worst. At the end of the
nineteenth century there were such writers as Robert
Louis Stevenson, who was sickly, and Oscar Wilde, who
was sickening. Nor should we overlook George Bernard
Shaw, who despite his beard gave us the word Shavian. Or
John Galsworthy, who in the *Forsyte Saga* proved how
many novels you can write about one family if you keep
at it.

Hurrying past A. E. Housman, who is best known for
saying "one-and-twenty" instead of "twenty-one," John
Masefield, who never recovered from a bad case of sea
fever, and William Butler Yeats, who if he had been Keats
would have pronounced his name Kates, we come to a
conclusion.[5]

---

[1] Trying to shake hands, Swinburne had got a thorn in his thumb.
[2] Our poet was obviously using a rhyming dictionary.
[3] It was an odd family. Swinburne also claimed that Sappho was his sister,
though she lived around 600 B.C.
[4] The reader may have begun to feel a little queasy too.
[5] English literature is not yet over, but the semester is.

IV
Shakespeare

It was a long time before they let me teach Shakespeare. People had to die or take another job, and I found that teachers of Shakespeare are invariably healthy and contented. In fact their happiness with their work may be why they are in such good health. If a statistical study were made, I think it would show that those who teach Shakespeare live eight or ten years longer than those who teach, say, Seventeenth-Century Prose or The Great Victorians.

By the time I taught Shakespeare it was almost too late. If I showed my delight in some of the more robust scenes and lines, I was thought a dirty old man, though I was barely forty. I was inclined to read aloud from the plays, changing my voice and mannerisms as I moved from character to character, and I thought I did almost as well as Maurice Evans or Sir John Gielgud. In a sense I did better, because these actors took only one part, whereas I could be Hamlet one moment and Polonius another, not to mention the Queen and Ophelia.

One of my colleagues who was teaching The Early Novel in the classroom across the hall said I was disturbing him. At about the same time I found written on the blackboard (the coward had printed it in large letters rather than reveal his or her handwriting) a message that took away much of my confidence as a Shakespearean actor. The message stated, very simply: "ARMOUR IS A HAM."

Though I began to read the great passages in more subdued tones, I did not allow these rebuffs to cool my ardor for Shakespeare. Occasionally I was so carried away that I shouted the soaring, passionate lines as dramatically as ever. I did, that is, until there was a tapping on my door and I could see dimly through the frosted glass the outline of a burly colleague, unable to teach Richardson and Sterne while I was King Henry V, rallying my followers against the French at Harfleur. Unless I could find a more remote classroom, I knew I would have to interpret the Bard less histrionically.

All of this is by way of indicating my love of Shakespeare, which some who have read a certain book of mine may doubt. In *Twisted Tales from Shakespeare* I am spoofing not Shakespeare but myself or some person who takes literally the figurative language of the poet and views unimaginatively the conventions of the theater. I am not parodying Shakespeare's plays but retelling them in my own irreverent way. In the general introduction, the introduction to each play, and the appendices I am also, I confess, having a little fun with the scholars and their clichés and mannerisms. Considerately, I mention no names.

I soon discovered that I could not make humor out of humor. I decided to leave the boisterous comedies alone, though I included one romantic, fanciful comedy, *A Midsummer Night's Dream,* among the six plays I chose to retell. I found I could do best with the great tragedies, since the more lofty the language the more incongruous was my lowbrow version; hence *Hamlet, Macbeth, Romeo and Juliet, The Merchant of Venice,* and *Othello.* I skipped *King Lear* because I was uncomfortable fooling around with pathos, though it could be done. The history plays, which also have their possibilities, I stayed away from because there are too many historical complications to handle in small space.

Above all, I wished to retell the plays most familiar to high school and college students. I therefore had no trouble deciding against *Cymbeline, Coriolanus,* and *Timon of Athens.* But soon after the book was published I began hearing from students who told me that I had left out a classroom favorite, *Julius Caesar.* So I included that one in *The Classics Reclassified.* By special request, you might say.

Now I have another decision to make. Since space permits inclusion of only one of the plays here, which shall it be? It must be the most-taught, most-studied, most-interpreted of Shakespeare's plays. And that, of course, is *Hamlet.* Omitting the introduction with which I preface it and the questions which follow it, in *Twisted Tales from Shakespeare,* here is my retelling of Shakespeare's masterpiece. I have done it no harm. It is too great to be harmed.

HAMLET

Hamlet Sees A Ghost

Hamlet, the Prince of Denmark, is known as the Melancholy Dane, capable of depressing anyone within sight or sound of him. The reason he mopes around all day is that his father has died and his father's brother has inherited both the throne and the Queen. Thus the new King, who had been Hamlet's uncle, is now his stepfather as well, and relations are becoming both strained and numerous. The King and Queen try to get Hamlet to stop mourning the death of his father and to take off his "inky cloak," on which as a student at Wittenberg he apparently kept wiping his pen. But Hamlet won't change either his clothes or his attitude.

Just after midnight one night, a guard named Francisco is walking on a platform in front of the castle so he will be in plain sight of any approaching enemy.

"Stand and unfold yourself," he cries out when a second guard, named Bernardo, approaches. Why Bernardo has folded is not explained, but the late hour might have something to do with it. Anyhow, Francisco has a right to be suspicious, for it turns out that Bernardo has come to relieve him of his watch.

Two other guards, Horatio and Marcellus, join the group, and their idle chatter turns to ghosts. Marcellus and Bernardo claim to have seen the ghost of the ex-King of Denmark, Hamlet's father, several nights running.[1] Horatio is a skeptic and won't be convinced until he sees the ghost with his own eyes.

The ghost promptly obliges, appearing in full armor, heavy though it is on his ectoplasm.

"Mark it, Horatio," whispers Bernardo, who has an orderly mind. But Horatio can't find a pencil, and isn't sure it would show on a ghost anyhow.

Horatio tries to engage the ex-King in conversation, but, never having passed the time of night with a ghost before, can think of nothing better than "Speak to me" (or, in some texts, "Spook to me"), which is a feeble opening gambit. Finally, after an awkward silence, the ghost hears a cock crow and clanks off. Horatio thinks that if anyone can get the ghost to talk it would be Hamlet, since blood is thicker than water.[2] So they go off to fetch him.

---

[1] And out of breath.

[2] And much thicker than whatever the ghost has in his veins.

Before they leave, Horatio cries, "Break we our watch up." He is obviously distraught.[1]

Hamlet, meanwhile, is in the castle, where the King and Queen are trying to cheer him up.

"How is it that the clouds still hang on you?" asks the King, who is interested in meteorological phenomena. But Hamlet is of no help, having majored in philosophy.

"Seek not for thy noble father in the dust," counsels the Queen, having noticed Hamlet poking around behind the furniture. But he goes on brooding, and running his finger along the tops of shelves.

After the King and Queen exeunt, which they do frequently, having been married only two months, Hamlet is left muttering to himself.

"O that this too too solid flesh would melt!" he groans. He has been dieting for weeks, trying to get into condition after going on a binge of Danish pastry.

The next night, having been told of the ghost by Horatio, Hamlet mounts the platform and takes his post, needing something to defend himself with. He is full of anticipation, never having seen the ghost of a close relative before, and somewhat uncertain about protocol. Promptly at midnight the ghost appears, his face looking so gray that Hamlet is about to ask him if he is ill, when he remembers. Taking Hamlet aside, he makes what is obviously a prepared speech.[2] The climax of it comes when he asks Hamlet to avenge his "foul and most unnatural murther."

"Murther?" Hamlet asks incredulously. He thinks the ghost must surely mean "mother," and this seems like strong language to use even about Gertrude.

"Murder," says the ghost, dropping the lisp, "murder

[1] Or else time means nothing to him.
[2] The original ghost-written address.

most foul." He goes on to say that it was he, Hamlet's father, who was murdered, and by none other than Hamlet's uncle.

"Uncle!" cries Hamlet at this point, but the ghost won't be stopped, and continues to describe every gruesome little detail. It seems that he had been catching forty winks in the garden when the murderer crept up and poured poison in his ears.[1] This way the victim was unable to detect the telltale taste and spit it out. Nor, with his ears awash, could he hear the murderer's departing footsteps. It looked like the Perfect Crime.

Having told his story, the ghost turns on his heel to get back to Hell before they call the roll.

"Whither ghost?" asks Hamlet, but gets no reply.

It is almost daybreak, and it dawns on Hamlet. He swears to have revenge on King Claudius for the dastardly deed, and to make his mark.[2]

"O, fie!" he swears, looking around first to be sure no ladies are present. "O, fie!"

When Horatio and Marcellus run in, Hamlet makes them swear on their swords, which they find ridiculous and uncomfortable, never to blab about what they have witnessed this night.

"Swear," puts in the ghost, who is under the platform, burrowing for all he's worth but making slow headway toward Hell and still able to take part in the conversation.

Before they leave the platform, Hamlet, Horatio, and Marcellus argue about the hour and try to synchronize their watches. "The time is out of joint," says Hamlet in disgust.

---

[1] Actually "in the porches of my ears" is what the ghost says. His ears must have been pretty sizable, with steps and everything.
[2] On King Claudius.

Hamlet Acts Crazy

Now Hamlet knows his father has been murdered by his uncle, but he has only a ghost's word for it, and this is pretty flimsy evidence.[1] He decides to get some more proof, and meanwhile to pretend he is off his rocker so as to catch the King off his guard. As long as he appears insane, he can act with impunity, a poniard, or anything else that comes to hand. He has no fear of being committed, a little insanity being expected of members of the royal family, whose parents were usually first cousins.

The first person he tries this out on is Ophelia, his girl friend, a sensitive creature who comes unhinged easily. Upset on finding her fiancé gone berserk overnight, she runs to tell her father, Polonius, a garrulous old windbag who is adviser to the King and to anyone else who will listen.

Bursting into Polonius' room, Ophelia looks as if she has seen a ghost. Actually she is one of the few who hasn't.

"How now, Ophelia, what's the matter?" asks Polonius. Her eyes are starting from their sockets and there's no telling where they will go if they aren't stopped. Polonius, an observant father, figures that something is amiss.

"My lord, as I was sewing in my closet," she begins, without explaining why she picked a place with such poor light, "Lord Hamlet, with his doublet all unbrac'd, no hat upon his head, his stockings fouled, ungarter'd, and down-gyved to his ankle, pale as his shirt, and his knees knocking each other, comes before me." At first she thought he was looking for the W.C. and had opened the wrong door. But when he grabbed her by the wrist and backed off at arm's length, she knew he was not his normal self. He had never backed off before.

---

[1] It wouldn't stand up in court, and any judge could see through it.

Polonius sizes up the situation at once.[1] "This is the very ecstasy of love," he says firmly. He knows all the symptoms: the hatlessness, the hopelessness, and the walking knock-kneed to try to keep the stockings up. His daughter has driven the Prince mad with desire, and he is rather proud of her.

"Come, go we to the King. This must be known," he tells Ophelia, hustling her off to the castle. Polonius loves to be a bearer of tidings, whether good or bad.[2]

In the castle the King and Queen are talking with two courtiers named Rosencrantz and Guildenstern, who in any other time would have been members of a comedy team or a law firm. The King, who hasn't yet heard Polonius' story, has noticed Hamlet acting strangely of late, and he asks R. and G., who have known him since boyhood, to do a little private detective work. When they agree, the King says, "Thanks, Rosencrantz and gentle Guildenstern," and the Queen says, "Thanks, Guildenstern and gentle Rosencrantz." Either they play no favorites or they can't tell the two men apart.

"I have found the very cause of Hamlet's lunacy," Polonius blurts out as he hurries up to the King.

"O, speak of that. That do I long to hear," begs the King, who loves nothing better than having someone talk to him about the mental aberrations of his kinfolk.[3]

"Since brevity is the soul of wit," Polonius begins, "I will be brief." The speech that follows, however, is neither short nor funny. It includes reading the full text of a love

---

[1] He gets the wrong size, as usual.
[2] Had he been a woman, Polonius would have been known as a gossipmonger. But adviser to the King was the male equivalent.
[3] There is evidence that the King once considered a career in psychiatry, but gave it up when there was a sudden vacancy on the throne.

letter from Hamlet to Ophelia in which Hamlet quotes a poem of his own composition which was apparently so statistical, perhaps enumerating Ophelia's charms, that it sickened even the author. ("I am ill at these numbers," is the way he puts it.) While Polonius is still talking, he sees Hamlet approaching and hustles the King and Queen out of the room.

"I'll board him," he says. Polonius board everybody.

Hamlet enters with his nose in a book.[1] Polonius, testing his sanity, asks him a searching question. "Do you know me, my lord?"

"Excellent well. You are a fishmonger," Hamlet answers, not even coming close.

As the questioning proceeds, Polonius becomes increasingly certain that Hamlet is out of his head because of unrequited love, which is one of the worst kinds. Actually, as we know, Hamlet is playing a part, which means that anyone who plays the part of Hamlet is really acting.

Rosencrantz and Guildenstern now come in to try to find out what is wrong with their old classmate. But Hamlet uses doubletalk, which they are unable to figure out even though there are two of them.

"I am but mad north-northwest," he says, peering at a compass and laughing eerily. "When the wind is southerly I know a hawk from a handsaw."[2] What he means is that he is only crazy when he wants to be, but R. and G. don't get it. They think Hamlet is addlepated and Hamlet thinks they have holes in their heads. He is nearer right than they are.

---

[1] So as not to lose his place.
[2] "Handsaw" is probably a corruption of "hacksaw" or "Hawkshaw" or something. Corruption was rife in those days.

Hamlet Is Tested Some More

Polonius still wants to prove to the King that Hamlet is mad about Ophelia. Yet busy as he is, barking up the wrong tree, he still has time to give advice. While his son, Laertes, is packing his bags to go to France, the helpful father stands by and hands him old saws.[1]

"Give every man thy ear, but few thy voice," he advises his son, knowing you can always get a hearing aid but vocal cords are irreplaceable. And "Neither a borrower nor a lender be," he counsels, hoping the lad will think twice before writing home for money.

Once Laertes is gone, Polonius goes back to minding Hamlet's business. He suggests to the King that they hide behind the arras and eavesdrop on Ophelia and Hamlet. "I'll loose my daughter to him," says Polonius, who has kept her on a leash ever since she became interested in boys.

While the King and Polonius are hiding behind the arras, Ophelia, the bait, walks up and down reading a book, although her heart isn't in it.

Hamlet comes in, looking ghastly, all "sicklied o'er with the pale cast of thought," and muttering to himself loud enough for people in the second balcony to hear.[2]

"To be or not to be," Hamlet says profoundly, making a simple statement sound so philosophical that it has led to hundreds of scholarly interpretations. Then he talks about suffering from slingshots and arrows, taking his arms out of the sea, shuffling off a coil, and making his quietus (a small carved object) with a bodkin.[3] Since he doesn't know anyone is listening, and has no reason to pretend, maybe he really *is* crazy.

---

[1] See "handsaw," above.
[2] The medical term for this sort of thing is a soliloquy.
[3] Whose bodkin? Od's?

"Good my lord," Ophelia greets him pleasantly, "how does your honor for this many a day?" It's his mental health she is interested in, but she asks about his honor so as not to be too obvious.

"I humbly thank you, well, well, well," Hamlet replies, his tongue getting caught in his teeth toward the end.

Ophelia is sweet and gentle with Hamlet, offering to return his old love letters. But he denies ever having written them. Even if he had, what would he want with old letters anyhow, he snarls. He's not collecting stamps.

Finally Hamlet screams at her, "Get thee to a nunnery," and stomps out. Ophelia is left with her memories and a pile of old letters. She is too innocent to think of blackmail or breach of promise.

As the King and Polonius come from behind the arras, the King says this doesn't look like love to him—anyway, not as he remembers it. He's also beginning to think that Hamlet's pate isn't addled after all, and that he has something else on his mind. Maybe he could be sent on a business trip to England, where his madness wouldn't be so noticeable. Anyhow, the sea air might clear his head or at least unstop his nasal passages. Hamlet's heavy breathing is beginning to worry the King.[1]

The Play within a Play

Hamlet, for his part, isn't growing any fonder of his uncle. "Bloody, bawdy villain! Remorseless, treacherous, lecherous, kindless villain" is the best he can say for him.

"He breaks my pate across, plucks off my beard and blows it in my face, and tweaks me by the nose," Hamlet exaggerates, "and I just sit here and take it." He is beginning to think there is something wrong with him inter-

---

[1] It keeps the tapestries in a constant flutter.

nally. "Methinks," he says clinically, "I am pigeon-livered."

An idea comes to him when he meets a troupe of actors who have just had a long run, although we are not told from where.[1] One of their plays, *Caviar to the General,* is about a high-ranking officer who was murdered with some tainted fish eggs. Hamlet decides to alter the script slightly to make it similar to the ghost's story, and then watch the King while the King watches the play.

But first Hamlet, who so far as we know has never done any acting, gives the players detailed advice on how to play their parts. "Speak the speech trippingly," he tells them, rolling an "r" back and forth across his tongue. The actors listen respectfully, whatever they may think,[2] because Hamlet is paying the bills.

So the play is put on. Part of it is a dumb show, and the rest of it is not much cleverer. To help the King get the idea, the actors hold up a sign reading: "Any resemblance to persons living and dead is purely intentional."

When they get to the point where a murderer pours poison into the sleeper's ears, the King's gorge rises.[3]

"Give me some light," he shouts, as if unable to read his program. His face is deathly pale, and the curl has gone out of his beard. Exit the King, sickened.

"Ah, ha!" Hamlet cries, half exulting and half laughing. When Rosencrantz and Guildenstern bring him word that the King is suffering from a sore throat caused by his choler, Hamlet knows that the ghost spake the truth about his father's murder.

" 'Tis now the very witching time of night," he mutters

---

[1] Probably from wherever they opened.
[2] Some think he is gargling.
[3] The king rises with it.

to himself, feeling the devilish impulse to go out and ring doorbells. Then, seized by a sudden thirst for a warming drink, he adds, "Now could I drink hot blood!"[1]

Hamlet Visits His Mother

Elsewhere in the castle the King is pacing about, taking steps to get rid of Hamlet. Finally he decides to pray. It might do some good, and it can't hurt. Or so he thinks until he tries to kneel.

"Bow, stubborn knees," he says, so accustomed to giving orders that he dictates to his own joints.

Hamlet, who is down the corridor a few hundred yards, hears the creaking and comes over to see what's up and who's down. The King is so busy trying to remember a prayer, any old prayer, that he doesn't notice his nephew-stepson (and would-be murderer), who stands right behind him with a naked sword.

"Now might I do it Pat," Hamlet says to some Irishman not listed among the characters.

But Hamlet is a man who can't act.[2] Besides, his mood has changed, and at this moment a cup of hot blood would be positively nauseating.

"Up, sword," he says to his well-trained blade. If killed now while praying, the King might go to Heaven, where Hamlet thinks he would spoil the tone of the place. Hamlet will wait until he is drunk, swearing, committing incest, or busy with one of his other pursuits.

At this point Hamlet is summoned to his mother's dressing room for a dressing down. What he doesn't know, unless he expects it as a matter of course, is that Polonius is hiding behind the arras,[3] taking down every

---

[1] But he had to go thirsty, all the blood banks being closed at that time of night.
[2] Unfortunately also true of many who play Hamlet.
[3] There seems to be an arras in every room in the castle. A waterproofed one is used as a shower curtain.

word.

"Hamlet, thou hast thy stepfather much offended," says the Queen, who is given to understatement.

Thereupon Hamlet brings out two snapshots that he just happens to have with him, one of the Queen's first husband (in his pre-ghost days) and one of her second, the present King. "See what a grace was seated on this brow," he says admiringly of the first, "Hyperion's curls, the front of Jove himself,[1] and an eye like Mars." As for the second, "This one," he sniffs, "looks like a mildewed ear." Either Hamlet is prejudiced or King Claudius had better replace the Court Photographer.

As Hamlet waxes excited over the comparison and waves the pictures wildly, the Queen grows frightened.

"What wilt thou do? Thou wilt not murder me? Help, ho!"

"What ho?" asks Polonius from his hiding place. He is slightly hard of hearing.

"Was that a rat?" asks Hamlet, noticing the rather squeaky voice. Without waiting for an answer, he whips out his sword and stabs Polonius through the arras.

To make the scene more confusing, the ghost of Hamlet's father now glides onstage in his nightgown, unable to sleep because of all the din. He looks more ghostly than he did in his armor.

"Do not forget! This visitation is but to whet thy almost blunted purpose," the ghost tells Hamlet, making motions as if to sharpen something. "But look, amazement on thy mother sits.[2] Speak to her."

"How is it with you, lady?" asks Hamlet politely.

"How's it with you?" she replies.

---

[1] Whose rear, he doesn't say.
[2] Chairs seem to be at a premium in this scene. See above, ". . . grace was seated on this brow."

74

Seeing that this sort of small talk isn't getting them anywhere, Hamlet apologizes to the Queen for making a hole in the draperies and drags the body of Polonius into another room. For once, Polonius hasn't a thing to say.

Ophelia Goes to Pieces

When the Queen tells her husband of Hamlet's wild behavior, and how he mistook Polonius for a rat, the King is upset. "Where is he now?" he asks worriedly.

"Gone to draw apart the body he hath killed," replies the Queen, apparently thinking that Hamlet is now dismembering poor old Polonius.

The King shudders. "Ho, Guildenstern!" he shouts, and in come both Rosencrantz and Guildenstern. The same thing would have happened if he had shouted, "Ho, Rosencrantz!" He orders them to take Hamlet to England. They are also to take sealed instructions to the King of that country, indicating that Hamlet is expendable.[1]

Once Hamlet is on his way to England, the King breathes easier, and breathing has always been a matter of considerable importance to him.

But he and the Queen get a nasty jolt when Ophelia comes in, singing off-key and strewing[2] flowers all over the place. The death of her father and the madness of her lover have lowered her I.Q. to a point where it can no longer be measured. To make matters worse, Laertes has suddenly returned from France and makes a scene (Scene V) because his father was buried before he could get to the funeral. Here they've spent all that money for mourners, when he would have done it for nothing.

Meanwhile Ophelia, not to be outdone, is singing "Hey

---

[1] In those days kings were always doing little things like this for each other.
[2] It is one of the oddities of the English language that everything else you throw, but flowers you strew.

non nonny, nonny, hey nonny," and other popular songs, and madly passing out flowers to everyone within reach. The King begins to wonder whether he has sent the right party to England.

"There's rosemary, that's for remembrance, and there's pansies, that's for thoughts,"[1] she says as she hands a few blooms to Laertes, not realizing how embarrassed the poor lad is, standing there with a bouquet in his hands. Then she deals out fennel and columbines to the King and daisies and rue to the Queen. "And here's some for me," she says, not wanting to leave anybody out. The poor girl may be pretty far gone, but she still knows her flowers. Even if she doesn't become Princess of Denmark, she would make a good Queen of the May.

The End of Ophelia[2]

Word comes to the King that Hamlet has got loose from Rosenstern and Guildencrantz and is headed home.

"To the quick of the ulcer," the King says crisply to Laertes, not wanting to beat around the abdomen. "What would you like to do to the fellow who has stabbed your father through the arras and driven your sister flower-strewing?"

"Cut his throat i' the church," snaps back Laertes, who visualizes the consternation of the preacher and the people in nearby pews.

"No," says the King soothingly. "There's a better way." Laertes has quite a reputation as a swordsman, and the King proposes that he engage Hamlet in a friendly bout in

---

[1] She is completely wacky, and so is her grammar.
[2] "There's a divinity that shapes our ends," said Hamlet once, in happier days, as he watched Ophelia walk gracefully away from him.

which Hamlet will be given a rapier with a blunt end, while Laertes will use a nice sharp blade with poison on the tip. In case anything goes wrong, they will offer Hamlet a poisoned drink to cool him off permanently. Laertes agrees, having nothing to lose but a few minutes of his time.

At this moment the Queen comes running in. She is upset by something, possibly Laertes' sword. "One woe doth tread upon another's heel," she says, as soon as she gets to her feet again. His sister, she tells Laertes, has gone to a watery grave, and must be moved to a cemetery on higher ground. It seems that Ophelia was hanging garlands on the limb of a willow tree, trying to improve on nature, when the limb broke and she fell into the brook. The Queen, a frustrated pulp writer, describes the scene vividly.

"Her clothes spread wide, and, mermaid-like, awhile they bore her up, which time she chanted snatches of old tunes." But then, she adds sorrowfully, "Her garments, heavy with their drinks,¹ pulled the poor wretch from her melodious lay to muddy death." Why the person who gave the Queen this detailed account didn't fish Ophelia out is not explained. Perhaps he knew the plot.

"Alas, then, she is drowned," exclaims Laertes, hazarding a guess.

"Drowned, drowned," the Queen says, sure enough of the result of long immersion to speak firmly and repetitiously.

"Too much of water hast thou, poor Ophelia, and therefore I forbid my tears," says Laertes, fearful of making things any soggier.

---

¹ They had obviously had one too many.

A Grave Situation

The last acts opens in a churchyard, where two jolly gravediggers are digging for comic relief. From time to time they lean on their spades and exchange witticisms. They seem to have grown calloused, especially on the palms. One gravedigger leaves for town to fetch a stoup of liquor, while the other, who feels sick to his stomach, sings dolefully as he digs, and now and then throws up a skull.[1]

Hamlet and Horatio enter the churchyard, and Hamlet exchanges pleasantries with the gravedigger, asking him, for instance, "How long will a man lie i' the earth ere he rot?"[2] One of the skulls Hamlet has been fiddling with turns out to have belonged to Yorick, the court jester, who used to let Hamlet ride on his back. Hamlet was attached to the fellow, and as he fondles the skull he grows nostalgic.

"Alas, poor Yorick," he sighs. The years have not been kind to his old friend.

Enters now a funeral procession, consisting of the King, Queen, Laertes, Mourners, and Ophelia. Everyone, except of course Ophelia, walks slowly, with downcast eyes. Hamlet and Horatio bend over a tombstone, pretending to be epitaph collectors. When the name of Ophelia is mentioned, Hamlet pricks up his ears.

"Lay her i' the earth," cries Laertes,[3] "and from her fair and unpolluted flesh may violets spring!" It seems appropriate that his sister should wind up as a flower bed.

Then, when Ophelia has been lowered into the grave, he jumps in with her and begs them to bury him too. "We are in this thing together," he says.

---

[1] An early instance of skulldiggery.

[2] The gravedigger's answer, in case you, too, have been wondering, is about eight or nine years.

[3] Dropping his n's, as usual.

Thereupon Hamlet, not to be outburied, jumps in also. "This is I, Hamlet the Dane!" he cries, so they will carve his name correctly on the headstone.

Laertes, angered at thus being upstaged—whose sister's funeral is this, anyway?—grapples with Hamlet. They fight at close quarters, there not being room for anything else.

"I prithee," gasps Hamlet, always polite, "take thy fingers from my throat."

"Pluck them asunder," orders the King, realizing that without poisoned daggers, et cetera, the wrong man might get killed. At last he convinces the two hotheads that they should get out of the hole they are in and fight a proper duel where the spectators will have a better view.

None of this has been helping Ophelia any.

The Duel

All the members of the court assemble to see the bout. It seems an uneven match, since Laertes is Champion of France and Hamlet isn't even ranked. What the odds-makers don't know is that Hamlet has been practicing for months, just on the chance of such an emergency. He is always expecting trouble, and isn't called the Melancholy Dane for nothing.

"There is special providence in the fall of a sparrow," says Hamlet apropos of nothing. And then, to prove he is good at wordplay, if not swordplay, he rattles off, "If it be now, 'tis not to come; if it be not to come, it will be now; if it be not now, yet it will come." When he concludes, the courtiers applaud enthusiastically. As an encore he runs through "Peter Piper picked a peck of pickled peppers."

At first Hamlet gets the better of Laertes, once touching

him on the button[1] with his rapier, whereupon trumpets blare and symbols clash.[2] The King begins to stir restlessly.[3] He offers Hamlet a drink, but Hamlet says he wants to finish the duel first. The King makes it sound so refreshing, however, that the Queen takes a hearty gulp herself, and immediately swounds. She isn't heard from again.

About the same time, Laertes sticks Hamlet with his poisoned blade. Then, in a clumsy bit of swordplay, the rapiers get switched and Laertes himself is inoculated.

"They bleed on both sides," comments Horatio, who is sitting up close and can check both the left side and the right.

Laertes, stretched out on the floor, has a sudden change of heart. "Hamlet," he cries, "thou art slain." This is a surprise to Hamlet, who is the one still on his feet. Laertes also tells him that the King is behind everything. Actually the King is only behind the throne, cowering, and Hamlet, stung at last to action, runs him through with the very weapon that the King himself has poisoned. It is ironical, and very sharp.

Hamlet is now aware of everything except that he is still alive. "I am dead, Horatio," he says sadly. And then, when Horatio is not convinced, he reverses the word order: "Horatio, I am dead."

After two more speeches, he has nothing further to say on the subject, and Horatio whispers, "Good night, sweet Prince," apparently thinking he has dozed off.

As a matter of fact, Hamlet is a gone goose, along with the King, the Queen, and Laertes. The place is a mess, with bodies, rapiers, and empty cups everywhere. It is

---

[1] Whether belly or collar is never made clear.
[2] Ever since, clashing symbols have been the curse of English literature.
[3] He wants to make sure the poison doesn't settle.

fortunate that at this moment Fortinbras, a Norwegian prince who is next in line for the throne now that they have run out of Danes, arrives on the scene to clear away the debris. The Court Undertaker couldn't have coped with so much business all at once.

Fortinbras orders a cannon shot off, aimed, it is hoped, over the heads of the audience. A final fanfare is sounded, and the play ends on a tragic note, usually ascribed to one of the trumpeters.

V
English Novel

A while back I wrote a piece entitled "Reading Habits of the Young." This is the way it began:

Once there was a high school teacher who got her students to read *Silas Marner* and enjoy it. She went about it in an unusual way. She told her students that it was a naughty book; that it was written by a woman named Mary Ann who preferred to be called George; and that they might get carried away by the story and miss the author's message. Her clincher was that it was available only in paperback.

The students read *Silas Marner* with such gusto that this teacher is thinking of trying the same technique with *Ivanhoe.*

The lesson to be derived from the above is that young people will read almost anything if it is not required, and if it is practically guaranteed not to do them any good.

I included both *Silas Marner* and *Ivanhoe* in *The Classics Reclassified,* and I thought of giving my version of one of them here. Each has the kind of excess that calls for my treatment, or mistreatment. *Silas Marner,* which I must admit held me enthralled when I first read it, is a bit lugubrious and melodramatic. As I point out in the opening of my retelling of it, "George Eliot wrote this moral tale to prove that everything comes out all right for nice people, at least in the novels of George Eliot."

As for *Ivanhoe,* a stirring tale of chivalry, full of romance and derring-do, the medievalism is laid on just a little too thick, both in language and in action. I say this, even while confessing that I was carried away by it in my youth, just as I was by *Silas Marner,* and I think everyone should read both books.

Why not, then, include my irreverent version of one of these slightly tattered classics here? The reason is that these books, which I read and enjoyed in my younger days, are no longer on the required reading list, or not with the inevitability they once were. I hope this is not because of what I have done to them. Perhaps some teachers do not require them because students might think them old hat. (Alas, I often find the old hat more becoming, and certainly more comfortable, than the new one.) At any rate, students and teachers tell me that *Silas Marner* and *Ivanhoe* are "out." That doesn't mean that they may not be "in" again one of these days.

One novel that is still assigned, in fact still read even if not assigned, is *David Copperfield.* It is such a rich, brimming-over novel, in its portrayal of London and its creation of characters, that it might seem impossible to be playful about it. But even the greatest literary works have their little defects. With *David Copperfield* these are sentimentality and, even better for my purpose, implausibility of plot. These, along with a few Dickensian eccentricities, are what I have worked on in the version that follows.

Before giving you *David Copperfield,* however, let me say something about the novel as a literary form. One dictionary definition describes a novel as "A fictitious prose tale of considerable length, in which characters and actions professing to represent those of real life are portrayed in a plot." Somehow that leaves out whatever it is that makes a novel like *David Copperfield* so readable and so enduring. Another dictionary definition tells us that a novel "usually deals with the passions, especially love." That comes a little closer, but it doesn't quite describe *David Copperfield* either, at least not the love part. If you are looking for explicit sex, this isn't the book for you.

Anyhow, teaching the novel is one of an English teacher's pleasantest tasks, and I sometimes wonder whether a teacher should be paid for it. Similarly, I wonder whether a student should get credit for doing something as enjoyable as reading novels. It is true that reading novels and taking a course in the novel are two quite different things, and what students have to put up with in a course, including tests and papers, may justify credit.

Now, on with *David Copperfield*. And forgive me, Charles Dickens.

DAVID COPPERFIELD

The story is told in the first person, by David Copperfield, though he is not born until the end of the first chapter. He has a remarkable memory, however, and remembers exactly how everyone looked and what everyone said during the argument between his mother, his aunt, and the doctor just before the delivery.

When David was born, he tells us, "The clock began to strike, and I began to cry, simultaneously." This probably does not mean that David was struck by the clock. However, it sets the tone of the book, in which somebody is always getting beaten and crying, although people frequently cry without being hit.

David's father died six months before David was born. This is the way he puts it: "My father's eyes had closed upon the light of this world six months when mine opened on it." Not only is this more delicate but it is recommended to any author who is being paid by the word. David's mother is a beautiful, baby-faced creature who married her late husband when she was half his age, which is probably why he called her his better half. Whenever anyone says a harsh word, her eyes fill with tears.[1]

David has a loyal friend in Peggotty, a plump nursemaid who is always hugging him and bursting the buttons off her dress. She is kept busy around the house, cooking, cleaning, and sewing on buttons.

Time passes. Once Peggotty takes David for a fortnight's visit to her brother's home, a fishing barge drawn up on dry land. It is almost as peculiar as the people in it. One of these is Peggotty's nephew Ham, whose name is wonderfully descriptive and whose laugh ("Hor! Hor!") is, fortunately, not contagious. Another is a Mrs. Gummidge, who speaks of herself as "a lone lorn creetur" and has a way of tugging at her own heart strings.

"Yon's our house, Mas'r Davy," says Peggotty as they approach, dropping two syllables for every one button. Among those David meets is Peggotty's niece, little orphan Em'ly, whose father has drownded and who feels sorry for all the poor fishermens and would like to help 'em if they was to come to any hurt. David falls in love with her immediately, doubtless fascinated by her bad grammar.

Returning home from the visit, David learns that his mother has married a Mr. Murdstone. As Peggotty tells him, with characteristic delicacy, "You have got a pa!" Thereupon, "Peggotty gave a gasp, as if she were swallowing something that was very hard." It is probably one of those Dickensian lumps in the throat.

---

[1] They are small, and fill rapidly.

Mr. Murdstone is tall, dark, handsome, and mean, and David takes an instant dislike to him. One senses the emergence of an Oedipus complex, but no reference is made to it, probably because Freud was born six years after the publication of *David Copperfield*.[1] Equally obnoxious is Murdstone's sister, Miss Murdstone, an uninvited guest who sits around stringing steel beads and urging her brother to be firm with David, which he has every intention of being.[2]

Mr. Murdstone, who wants his stepson to be well educated, tries to beat David's lessons into him, using a cane instead of a book.

"Mr. Murdstone, sir!" cries David, polite even under stress, "don't, pray don't beat me!" Then, forgetting his manners, he bites the hand that beats him, and Mr. Murdstone is left with a scar that is going to be hard to explain.

So David is sent off to a boarding school near London, driven by a carrier[3] named Barkis. It is this gentleman who is responsible for the Famous Quotation, "Barkis is willin'," which is his romantic way of sayin' that he has no serious objections to marryin' Peggotty. He keeps waitin' and hopin'.

At the school, Salem House, David falls in with a student with the odd name (in anything but a book by Dickens) of Tommy Traddles and another named J. Steerforth. Steerforth is extremely popular, since he has influence with the headmaster, Mr. Creakle. He talks back to the teachers and even causes one of them, a rather decent chap, to be dismissed. A pupil of many accomplishments,

---

[1] Oedipus, however, had been around for centuries, and Dickens missed the scoop of a lifetime.

[2] Miss Murdstone, according to one critic, is "cut of the same cloth" as Madame Defarge, in *A Tale of Two Cities*. It is tough material.

[3] Whether of mail or typhoid, we are never told.

Steerforth is unquestionably a forerunner of Progressive Education.

Time passes.[1] One day David is summoned home because of the death of his mother, which makes him a full-fledged orphan, like Oliver Twist and many another Dickens youngster who goes on to better things. The funeral is suitably depressing, but the most gruesome episode is when, as David says, "Miss Murdstone, who was busy at her writing-desk ... gave me her cold fingernails, and asked me, in an iron whisper, if I had been measured for mourning."[2] Miss Murdstone's detachable and refrigerated fingernails were a gift that should have delighted any red-blooded boy, but David does not so much as say thank-you.

Peggotty now takes David off to live with her kin, including little Em'ly, who is not so little as before and has soft "cherry lips," which go nicely with her apple cheeks. Peggotty and the persistent Barkis get married, because by now Peggotty also is willin'.

David is happy walking on the beach with little Em'ly, who looks up at him through her stray curls, blushing prettily. But Mr. Murdstone puts an end to this idling by sending the lad to London, to wash bottles for the firm of Murdstone and Grinby. It is not David's idea of a promising career,[3] and he is so unhappy that, as he says, "I mingled my tears with the water in which I was washing the bottles." Whether the solution was fifty-fifty, or nearer sixty-forty, he fails to say.

While working at Murdstone and Grinby's, David lives with a Mr. and Mrs. Micawber. Mr. Micawber is so oppressed by financial troubles that one night he comes

---

[1] It has to, because the novel covers about thirty years.
[2] What a chance this gave David to reply, "No, ma'am, nor for evening either."
[3] All he can see is bottlenecks.

home to supper "with a flood of tears," wearing a life preserver, no doubt. At such a sight David himself is "dissolved in tears," and shortly afterward they are all so overcome that, says David, referring to Mr. and Mrs. Micawber, "he mingled his tears with hers and mine." It is easily the dampest scene in English literature until Somerset Maugham's *Rain*.

Mr. Micawber, though in and out of debtor's prison, is always sure that one of these days "something will be turning up." At heart an optimist, he smiles while he weeps, and goes around with a salty taste in his mouth.

When the Micawbers move to another city and David has no one to cry with, he decides not to wash another bottle for Murdstone and Grinby but to run away to his Aunt Betsey Trotwood's in Dover. Thereupon ensues a harrowing journey in which the impoverished lad sells first his waistcoat and then his jacket and is lucky to get to Dover with his trousers.

At Miss Trotwood's, David comes to know Mr. Dick, who is even queerer than the usual Dickens character. Mr. Dick lives upstairs and likes to fly kites. He also has an obsession about King Charles the First's head, or perhaps it is King Charles's first head. Whatever it is, it keeps getting into the Memorial he is writing and prevents his completing it, which is about as good an excuse as an unpublished author has ever been able to think up.

Miss Trotwood, who is too busy chasing donkeys off her lawn to have time for tutoring her nephew, sends him to Doctor Strong's school in Canterbury. There he boards with Mr. Wickfield,[1] a lawyer who drinks port all evening and has to be shown to his bedroom by his daughter Agnes who, being a teetotaler, always knows the way. Mr. Wickfield's assistant in the law office is Uriah Heep, who

---

[1] If you think the characters are beginning to pile up confusingly, just wait.

is continually grinding the palms of his cold, clammy hands against each other "as if to squeeze them dry and warm, besides often wiping them, in a stealthy way, on his pocket handkerchief." Anyone who anticipates shaking hands with Uriah would be well advised to carry a towel. Uriah is forever describing himself as "a very umble person," dropping his eyes and his h's indiscriminately.

One evening after David has had dinner with Uriah and his mother ("Thanks Heeps," he says as he leaves), whom does he see but Mr. Micawber walking by! A few days later he runs across his old schoolmate, J. Steerforth, at an inn! England was very small in those days, or the laws of probability had not yet been passed.

Taking Steerforth with him, David, who is now an outstanding upstanding understanding young man of seventeen, goes to see his friend Peggotty. At first she fails to recognize him, but when she does, she cries out, "My darling boy!" and the next moment they are locked in a soggy embrace. It is just like old times.

The big news in the family is that Em'ly is affianced to Peggotty's nephew, the rough-hewn, thick-sliced Ham. A shadow is momentarily cast over the happy scene by Martha, a soiled woman who has been shadowing Em'ly, hoping to remind her of their days of innocence together and perhaps to get enough money to leave town. Martha is truly pathetic, covering her face to hide the ravages of Sin and making "a low, dreary, wretched moaning in her shawl" until Ham, who can stand it no longer, gives her his life's savings. At this point Em'ly, too, sobs hysterically, overcome either by Martha's plight or by her husband-to-be's depleted bank account.

But back to David. It is time for him to think of a career, and his Aunt Betsey suggests that he become a proctor, a profession which he is immediately enthusiastic about, though neither he nor the reader knows precisely what it is. At any rate, he is to be articled to the firm of Spenlow and Jorkins, in London, and must pay a thousand pounds for the privilege. David's reaction to this drain on his aunt's resources is so beautifully and unnaturally put that the passage should be quoted in full.

"Now, my dear aunt," he says, "I am uneasy in my mind about that. It's a large sum of money. You have expended a great deal on my education, and have always been the soul of generosity. Surely there are some ways in which I might begin life with hardly any outlay, and yet begin with a good hope of getting on by resolution and exertion."[1] This causes his aunt to explain, in a couple of hundred well-chosen words, why she will be only too happy to spend the thousand pounds on her nephew.[2] Whereupon, overcome by a wave of restraint, they neither embrace nor burst into tears.

David's aunt sets him up in elegant quarters in London, where under the influence of Steerforth and liquor he becomes (dare we use the word?) drunk. Attending the theater in this deplorable condition, he has the bad luck to sit right behind Agnes Wickfield, who has come to London, gone to the theater, and chosen this very seat, all for the sake of Dickens's plot.

"Lordblessmer! Agnes!" exclaims David thickly. He thinks he has ruined himself with Agnes, but that dear creature forgives him and invites him to dinner, no doubt to sober him up. She warns him against associating with that Bad Influence, Steerforth, and also tells him that Uriah Heep has her inebriated father in his power and is about to become a partner in the firm. In fact, as David

---

[1] One way would be to set up a school of education, where he might offer a course in How to Lay It On Thick.

[2] The reader can probably think of better ways for her to spend her money, such as building a fence around the lawn to keep off the donkeys.

learns later from Uriah's own unlovely lips, that slimy individual hopes to win Agnes also.

"Was it possible?" David asks himself, "that she was reserved to be the wife of such a wretch as this?" It is his first inkling that young women can be reserved, like seats at a theater, and he resolves to look into it.

David is invited for a weekend at the home of one of his employers, Mr. Spenlow, of Spenlow and Jorkins. Sure enough, Mr. Spenlow has a beautiful daughter, Dora, and sure enough, David falls in love with her. And who do you suppose is Dora's tutor? None other than Miss Murdstone, who has to get back into the story somehow. Forgetting about Em'ly and Agnes, David now can think of nothing but Dora. "I lived principally on Dora and coffee," he says, and becomes terribly lovesick, though it might be heartburn. His housekeeper, Mrs. Crupp, a dialect character who says "adwise" and calls David "Mr. Copperfull," tries in vain to cheer him up, or at least get him to eat something nourishing.

Now David's old schoolmate, Tommy Traddles, reappears, and so do Mr. and Mrs. Micawber, who are never more than a couple of chapters away. To David's distress, Mr. Micawber involves Traddles in a financial debt by using his name. Why anyone would want to use the name Traddles, even for monetary gain, is more than the reader can understand.

A great loss comes to David. Barkis dies. Or, as Dickens, writing fluidly, puts it, "It being low water, he went out with the tide." Another blow comes with the discovery that Em'ly has run off with Steerforth, who is now seen in his true colors (black and yellow). David is miserable, his heart being, as he says, "overcharged" with grief. There is nothing like being overcharged, unless it is being shortchanged, to bring on a fit of despondency.

But David is not in low spirits for long. He goes on a picnic with Dora, and when she presses his bouquet "against her little dimpled chin," David is driven into a series of the shortest and simplest declarative sentences in all Dickens: "I don't know how I did it. I did it in a moment. I had Dora in my arms. I was full of eloquence. I never stopped for a word. I told her how I loved her. I told her I should die without her. I told her that I idolized and worshiped her." Rather than hear any more of this, Dora consents to becoming engaged, and the reader is everlastingly grateful to her.

But alas, just as things are going well for David, Miss Trotwood arrives at his chambers and announces that she has been ruined (financially). David, just to prove he is human, is downcast by the news that his aunt can no longer support him.

At this point, as if Dickens had somehow contrived it, Agnes rides up in a hackney-chariot. As David says, trying to get out the words before the lump in his throat renders him speechless: "A fair hand was stretched forth to me from the window, and the face I had never seen without a feeling of serenity was smiling on me." Good old Agnes! A friend in need! Though she reports that her father is now completely in the toils of Uriah Heep, who has become a full partner, she knows of a job for David. It seems that his old schoolmaster, Dr. Strong, last heard of seventeen chapters back, at this very moment is in need of a secretary who can work mornings and evenings—precisely the time David has available from his articling with Spenlow and Jorkins. What incredible luck!

"I was pretty busy now," David reports after taking this second job, "up at five in the morning, and home at nine or ten at night." But, to speed the day he can afford to wed dear, dear Dora, he decides to study shorthand between midnight and 5 A.M.[1] His friend Traddles optimistically tells him that "it might be attained, by dint of perseverance, in the course of a few years."

Things now going better, we can be sure they will shortly go worse. Miss Murdstone, who fancies herself a private eye, discovers David's impassioned letters to Dora and reveals to Mr. Spenlow that this upstart hireling dares to love his daughter. The ambitious cad! Mr. Spenlow thereupon gives David a tongue-lashing, leaving him with welts across his psyche. Miss Murdstone, who would have loved bearbaiting, looks on in happy silence, though once she "laughs contemptuously in one short syllable." Dickens does not say whether it was "Ha," "Hee," or "Ho."

But the haughty Mr. Spenlow gets his. That very night, though there has been no previous hint of ill health, he drops dead. Still more shocking, his personal records reveal that he is not rich, after all! At one stroke (the one suffered by her father) Dora becomes (a) poor, and (b) an orphan like everyone else.

At this point let us quote the critic who said, "The plot of *David Copperfield*, to the student who compares it with most modern fiction, may seem almost incoherent." It will be seen, in what remains, that the word "almost" can be safely ignored.

For now, one snowy night in London when David is walking home, he almost bumps into—Em'ly's uncle!

"Well met, well met," the old fellow says repetitiously.

"Well met," answers David, who has a gift for mimicry. Inasmuch as Em'ly's uncle has been wandering all over England, France, Italy, and Switzerland, looking for his niece and that blackguard Steerforth, it is truly extraordinary that he should find David instead.

But back to David and Dora. They are wed and live

---

[1] The reader who puts in only a forty-hour week should feel ashamed of himself.

idyllically, she calling him Doady (having given up trying to pronounce David) and he calling her Child Wife and Little Blossom (having given up his brains). To anyone but the young newlyweds, it is all a little nauseating. David, having mastered shorthand, is now writing a book, dictating to himself at top speed. Dora, pretending to be his secretary, sits on his knee and holds his spare pens. With her precious curls and big blue eyes, she is as attractive a pen holder as you will ever see.

But what of Em'ly? She is found at last, and none too soon, because only a few chapters remain. She has left Steerforth, having learned after a few years that he was the rotter everyone else knew him to be in a few minutes. Her uncle finds her in London at Soiled Martha's, being browbeaten by Rosa Dartle, an old flame of Steerforth's who has loved him ever since the time he gallantly hit her in the mouth with a hammer. She has a disdainful way of speaking and a "curled lip." (See hammer blow, above.)

"What is there in common between *us?*" asks Rosa scornfully, wondering that Steerforth could have cared for both of them in the same delightfully brutal way.

"Nothing but our sex," says Emily. With this single candid observation, Dickens all but leaves the ranks of Victorian novelists. Anyhow, Em'ly is now back in the bosom of her family.

"Our future life lays over the ocean," says her uncle, telling Miss Trotwood of his plans for Em'ly and himself.

"They will emigrate together, aunt," David translates helpfully.

Disclosures and deaths now come thick and fast.[1] Mr. Micawber, who has been clerking for Uriah Heep, learns

---

[1] This is called the denouement, or "final disentangling of the intricacies of a plot." In Dickens it is usually the longest part of the book, there being so much to untangle.

that Uriah has forged Mr. Wickfield's name and made off with Miss Trotwood's money. When confronted with his crimes, Uriah ceases being umble and, as David remarks, "throws off his mask." Without his mask, he looks worse than ever.

Back now, for the last time, to Dora. She is sickening and has to be carried up and down stairs. It is a strain on the reader and on David's back. Before long she dies ("a Blossom that had withered in its bloom"), and at the very same instant her dog Jip keels over. In view of all the other coincidences, this double demise is not to be deemed extraordinary.

In fact it is more than matched by a succeeding incident, when Ham loses his life in attempting to rescue a man from a shipwreck, and the man, whose corpse is washed up on the shore, turns out to be (no it *couldn't* be) (but it is)—Steerforth! David, by the way, happens to be on the beach at the moment, though it is his first time at the seashore in years. It is a bit of luck, for no one else could have identified the long-absent Steerforth, who is in no condition to speak for himself.

David goes abroad for three years, mailing back to England the articles and books his course in shorthand has enabled him to write. All of them are gratefully accepted by publishers, probably because they are eager to get the foreign stamps for their collection. Returning home, rich and famous, he discovers to his amazement that he loves Agnes. He is even more amazed to find that Agnes loves him, too. It is the most amazing chapter in the book.

"I folded her to my heart," David says, first reading the directions and carefully observing the dotted lines.

Happiness comes at last to David Copperfield. There would seem to be no more need for tears. But Dickens is not ready to throw in the towel, damp though it is.

"Agnes," says David, "laid her head upon my breast and wept; and I wept with her, though we were so happy."

Although two chapters remain, let us leave them crying happily together and tiptoe away.

VI
Great Poets

Teaching poetry has one advantage over teaching prose: there is more to explain. You can go into such matters as rhyme, meter, blank verse, free verse, assonance, consonance, alliteration, imagery, personification, stanzaic patterns, odes, elegies, sonnets, pastorals, ballads, epics, and dramatic monologues, not to mention (but you must be sure to mention them) similes, metaphors, run-on lines, caesuras, and, if you want to pour it on, *vers de société* and such exotic forms as the *chant royal, kyrielle, pantoum, lai,* and *virelai.*

But the best thing about poetry, to a teacher, is the chance to tell students what a poem, or a specific line, is about, assuming the poet had something in mind. Of course the teacher may, when cornered, simply shrug and quote Archibald MacLeish's "A poem should not mean/ But be." The only trouble is that some student may ask, "What did MacLeish mean by that?"

I have taught poetry much more than prose and have learned all, or almost all, the tricks. It was many years before I discovered that provocative question, "What do *you* think?" I picked it up from a colleague who was known for his ability to stimulate discussion. If, while asking it, the teacher can put on a concerned, curious expression (an expression full of curiosity, that is), so much the better. While the question is being answered, the expression should reflect concentration, astonishment, skepticism, and grudging agreement, in that order, with just the right amount of pursing the lips, letting the mouth fall wide open, wrinkling the brow, and finally vigorously nodding the head. My colleague was not in English, but in History. If well handled, "What do *you* think?" seems to be effective in any field. But I myself have found it most useful in the teaching of poetry.

The great poets have inspired me to a form of collaboration. Tampering, some might call it, and they could be right. I feel, however, that the great poet and I are working together to produce something that requires more than one writer.

I began this some years ago when I fooled around a little with one of Wordsworth's Lucy Poems, "She Dwelt Among the Untrodden Ways." The first two stanzas I left untouched. The third stanza I altered only slightly, changing one word in the second line and one in the fourth. The whole poem is Wordsworth's, then, except for two words. Perhaps this is the way Wordsworth actually wrote it and there was a typographical error, or there were two errors. What I am sure of is that the poem takes on a new meaning, or a new relevance. Here is the revised poem:

LUCY REVISITED

She dwelt among the untrodden ways
Beside the springs of Dove,
A Maid whom there were none to praise
And very few to love:

A violet by a mossy stone
Half hidden from the eye!
—Fair as a star, when only one
Is shining in the sky.

She lived unknown, and few could know
When Lucy ceased to stir;
But she is in her grave, and, oh,
The difference to her!

My collaboration with Wordsworth emboldened me to work with other poets of the past. Instead of contributing only two words to a poem, however, I substituted an entire line of my own for the last line of a famous quatrain. This meant that I was now writing a fourth of the quatrain, or that the great poet and I were pooling our efforts in a ratio of three to one. My responsibility was therefore greater than it had been with Wordsworth, and I must try hard not to let my partner down.

I worked closely with such poets as Longfellow:

Lives of great men all remind us
We can make our lives sublime,
And, departing, leave behind us
Things unpaid for, bought on time.

And Henley:

Out of the night that covers me,
Black as the Pit from pole to pole,
I thank whatever gods may be
I have not stumbled in a hole.

And Tennyson:

Come into the garden, Maud,
For the black bat, night, has flown.
Come into the garden, Maud—
Don't bring a chaperon.

The next step was to work on a fifty-fifty basis, share and share alike. I took a single famous line and in place of the poet's next line added an infamous line of my own. The result was a book called *Punctured Poems,* illustrated by Eric Gurney, himself famous for *How to Live with a Neurotic Dog* and other works of high literary quality. I thought an artist who liked dogs would also like doggerel, and I was right. Our partnership on *Punctured Poems* led us to do *The Strange Dreams of Rover Jones* together, a book that has no connection with the study of English or American literature but is important to everyone concerned about caninity.

Two things were essential in selecting the famous lines I was to cap, or capsize. First they should be truly famous, or at least well known. Second, they should serve as a springboard for the plunge into the line which was my half of the couplet. To find such lines I went through Bartlett's *Familiar Quotations,* which in my edition is 1831 double-column pages of fine print, three times. I also perused numerous anthologies of poetry. It was harder to find just the right lines than you might suppose.

As I say in the Foreword to the book: "No apologies are made for the infamous second lines. Some of them will seem better when read over and over. At least they will approximately offset the number of lines which seem worse. If the reader is still unhappy, he can cross out the offending line and write something of his own—if it is not a borrowed copy." This might, in fact, be a good class exercise. Another would be to try to recall what the poet's own second line is. Better still, ask someone else what it is, having first looked it up yourself, and enjoy a moment of superiority.

Here are a few couplets, half man and half beast, from *Punctured Poems,* occasionally with a learned footnote.

Christopher Marlowe, "Dr. Faustus"

> Was this the face that launch'd a thousand
> ships?
> No wonder there are keel marks on her lips.[1]

William Shakespeare, "The Tempest"

> Full fathom five thy father lies.
> I pushed him. I apologize.

Alexander Pope, "Essay on Criticism"

> To err is human, to forgive divine.
> Some errors I forgive, though, quickly.
> . . . Mine.[2]

Percy Bysshe Shelley, "The Cloud"

> I bring fresh showers for the thirsting flowers.
> I've stood in the sun, with a hose, for hours.[3]

Samuel Taylor Coleridge, "The Rime of the Ancient Mariner"

> Water, water, everywhere;
> The plumbing badly needs repair.

Robert Browning, "My Last Duchess"

---

[1] Helen of Troy is said to have had a full lower lip. Apparently it was full of bolts and barnacles.
[2] And then there is Charles Townsend Copeland's "To eat is human; to digest, divine."
[3] See also Thomas Edward Brown's
  A garden is a lovesome thing, God wot,
  But only if God wotters it a lot.

That's my last Duchess painted on the wall.
I've scraped, but cannot get her off at all.

Omar Khayyám, "Rubáiyát" (tr. by Edward Fitzgerald)

A jug of wine, a loaf of bread, and thou. . . .
I'm not so very hungry anyhow.[1]

Henry Wadsworth Longfellow, "Paul Revere's Ride"

One if by land, and two if by sea. . . .
Now what do I do? He signals three!

Dante Gabriel Rossetti, "The Blessed Damozel"

The blessed damozel leaned out.
"She's sick!" I heard a warning shout.

Edna St. Vincent Millay, "Figs from Thistles"

My candle burns at both ends.
Where can I set it down, my friends?

T. S. Eliot, "The Hollow Men"

We are the hollow men.
It's time to eat again.[2]

After you have studied and taught the great poets and

---

[1] In the same poem we also have:
   The moving finger writes and, having writ,
   Is badly stained with ink, you must admit.
[2] Or, in view of the capital in some texts:
   We are the Hollow men:
   Fred Hollow, Bert Hollow, Ben.

come to look on them as friends, there is an element of sharing and intimacy in working with them in this way. It is an indescribable feeling which I shall not attempt to describe.

VII
American
Literature

I wonder whether you have read Nathaniel Ward's *The Simple Cobbler of Aggawam* recently. I read it once (but not more than once) and wrote a term paper on it in an American literature course in graduate school. The point I tried to make was that *The Simple Cobbler of Aggawam,* published in 1647, was the first humorous book written in America. I don't remember what grade I got on that paper, or what comment, and perhaps it is just as well. Why I thought a 69-year-old Puritan minister in Massachusetts in 1647 would write a funny book, I don't know. It may reveal to what lengths a student will go who is desperate for a subject.

Humor was slow starting in America. You won't find much of it in the works of Anne Bradstreet or Michael Wigglesworth (try *The Day of Doom* for laughs) or Cotton Mather or Jonathan Edwards. Sometimes I think the Puritans did not come to this country for freedom of worship but were expelled from England because they were so humorless.

Some literary historians believe that humor in American literature began with the Revolutionary songs and ballads, the bawdier ones made up by soldiers away from the restraining influence of wives and children. Something of the same sort, according to this theory, happened among hardy frontiersmen during the westward movement, and ultimately produced America's greatest humorist, Mark Twain.

However I am not now concerned with humor in American literature but with humor applied to American literature. If I have turned some sacred cows into bum steers, I am sorry, but not very. You have to be in the mood for this sort of thing. Coleridge writes of "the willing suspension of disbelief," necessary if the reader is to go along with such a work as *The Rime of the Ancient Mariner.* I probably should ask for "the willing suspension of seriousness." It might be worth mentioning that Coleridge himself wrote some parodies of overdone and underdone poetry. He published them under the name of Nehemiah Higginbottom, though he later, in his *Biographia Literaria,* confessed to authorship. At least I have not taken refuge in a pen name.

And now we come to *American Lit Relit,* which would seem to fit nicely into this survival kit because it is subtitled "A short history of American literature for long-suffering students, for teachers who manage to keep one chapter ahead of the class, and for all those who, no longer being in school, can happily sink back into illiteracy." That should take care of anyone who has read this far or has skipped the preceding chapters and started here.

American Lit Relit also carries what is called an "Author's Note." Such a title would indicate that I wrote it myself, which I did. It reads, and it comes out the same way if you read it yourself: "There are no half-truths in this book, but the reader may occasionally come upon a truth-and-a-half." Some pages back, in the first chapter, I quoted an essay, "Not Even Half Trying," in which I noted our preoccupation with the word "half." I forgot that I had been guilty of this myself, in the aforementioned Author's Note. Sometimes, I now realize, the reader may come upon a quarter-truth, which is only half a half-truth, or a truth-and-a-tenth, which is very slightly more than what is often called the whole truth. Whether a half-truth is the same as a half-falsehood, I do not know, but I think it should be.

Enough of mathematics, which is not my field. Let me now reduce *American Lit Relit* to a size, considerably less than half (closer to a fifth), that will fit in here. The book has already reduced its author, if not its subject, to absurdity.

THE BEGINNINGS OF AMERICAN LITERATURE

The first writers in America were probably Indians, writing for "little" magazines made of pieces of birch bark and being paid so much wampum per word. If one could leaf through one of these early journals, one might pick up some interesting ideas.[1] But all, alas, are gone, traded to white settlers as firewood in exchange for firewater. Other early writings, in the form of smoke signals, have fared no better. Efforts to deposit them in libraries led to poor visibility, fits of coughing, and mass resignations by cataloguers.

CAPTAIN JOHN SMITH

Captain John Smith was a professional soldier in his youth. He became a writer when "he exchanged his sword for a pen." Whether he had been trying unsuccessfully to dip his sword into an inkwell we do not know, but he was obviously a poor trader.

Captain John Smith's greatest contribution to American

---

[1] And no telling what else.

literature was his story, in *The Generall Historie of Virginia,* of how he was captured by the Indian leader, King Powhatan, and saved from having his brains beaten out when Pocahontas, the King's favorite daughter, "got his head in her armes, and laid her owne upon his to save him from death." It was a touching scene, her head touching his, and many doubt it ever happened. Captain John Smith may not have invented the short story, but he made an important contribution to the tall tale.

WILLIAM BYRD

Most of Byrd's writings were in the form of diaries, which caused him to be referred to as "the American Pepys."[1] His use of capitals is somewhat perplexing, as when he writes, "We all kept Snug in our several apartments till Nine, except Miss Thecky, who was the Housewife of the Family." The reader at first thinks Snug is a dog or a cat, a favorite of everyone. This same Miss Thecky turns up in Byrd's description of a walk he took on Governor Spotswood's estate: "Just behind was a cover'd Bench, where Miss Thecky often sat and bewail'd her Virginity." Interestingly, she lamented not the loss of it but still having it. This, it must be remembered, was the South, not New England.

EARLY NEW ENGLAND WRITERS

William Bradford wrote his *Of Plimouth Plantation* in what he called "a plaine stile." The following is an example of his plaine stile and fancy spellinge: "Some became souldiers, others took upon them farr viages." A farr viage was probably the same as a longg trippe.

Governor John Winthrop's *Journal* is full of accounts

---

[1] So far as is known, Pepys has never been called "the English Byrd."

of the evils and afflictions dear to the heart of a Puritan. Describing the murder of a nice old planter by a band of Indians, Winthrop wrote: "They found John Oldham stark naked, his head cleft to the brains, and his hands and legs cut as if they had been cutting them off, and yet warm." Had the rescuers arrived a few minutes earlier, they would have witnessed a lively scene, forsooth.

One writer who was not a Puritan was Thomas Morton. The revelry of Morton and his friends around a Maypole, tossing flowers into the air and performing other pagan rites, was shocking to behold.

But he was not as bad as Roger Williams, who was forced to flee to Rhode Island because he had such radical ideas as belief in tolerance, independent thinking, and kindness to Indians. He was born too soon.[1]

BAY PSALM BOOK

Poetry began with the *Bay Psalm Book*, of which only a few copies have survived. It is possible, by examining the word order of such lines as

> The Lord to mee a shepheard is,
> Want therefore shall not I,

to guess why.

ANNE BRADSTREET

Anne Bradstreet collected her poems in a volume called *The Tenth Muse, Lately Sprung up in America*.[2] The rest of the title, containing such phrases as *Severall Poems, compiled with great variety of Wit and Learning, full of*

---

[1] In fact he would have been born too soon if he were living today.
[2] Some think it should be *Strung up*.

111

delight, was, in later editions, transferred to the jacket as a blurb. One of Mrs. Bradstreet's poems contains these lines descriptive of her husband:

> My head, my heart, mine Eyes, my life, nay more,
> My joy, my Magazine of earthly store.

Her husband, overwhelmed, expired shortly thereafter.

MICHAEL WIGGLESWORTH

A name to be reckoned with, and not easily forgotten, is Michael Wigglesworth. In *The Day of Doom* his purpose was to terrify sinners, and he succeeded admirably. Probably the most memorable part of the poem describes the damnation of infants who died before they had time to become regular churchgoers. These tiny tots "from womb unto the tomb were straightway carried," according to Wigglesworth, who could not help admiring an efficient funeral arrangement.

LATER EARLY NEW ENGLAND WRITERS

Colonial literature was greatly influenced, though not necessarily for the better, by the Mathers. Their names were Increase and Cotton, not to be confused with Decrease and Dacron.

INCREASE MATHER

Increase Mather, a man of average size who was always drawing himself up to his full height, was the author of *An Essay for the Recording of Illustrious Providences.* Interestingly, all of these Providences were in Massachusetts, no mention being made of the one in Rhode Island. President of Harvard for sixteen years, he not only believed in demons but took part enthusiastically in the Salem witch trials, thus proving that education need be no handicap.

COTTON MATHER

Cotton Mather, Increase's son, entered Harvard at the age of eleven and was too light for the football team. When he failed to succeed his father as president of Harvard, it grieved him sorely. In a fit of pique, he founded Yale.

THE NEW ENGLAND PRIMER

All New England books were prim, but this one was primmer.

SAMUEL SEWALL

One of the most interesting entries in Sewall's *Diary* has to do with an Indian who, apparently on a whim, or a dare, hanged himself in the Brewhouse, whereupon "The Coroner sat upon him, having a jury, and ordered his burial by the highway with a stake through his grave." This graphic picture of the coroner and the jury sitting on the dead Indian until he could be buried is as memorable as anything in Colonial literature.

JONATHAN EDWARDS

Jonathan Edwards' greatest sermon was "Sinners in the Hands of an Angry God." It was sure-fire, as well as hell-fire, depicting an eternity of damnation so vividly that after a few minutes he had his parishioners emptying their pockets into the collection plate and writhing on the floor. At heart a kindly man, Edwards withstood the urge to horsewhip them while they were in this helpless position.

BENJAMIN FRANKLIN

A great change in American literature came with Benjamin Franklin. Unlike Jonathan Edwards, who believed in saving souls, the more practical Franklin believed in saving money. Ben was the son of a candle-maker in Boston, and from him he learned how foolish and wasteful it is to burn your candle at both ends.

His *Autobiography*, which today would be entitled *How to Become Rich and Famous through Hard Work*, was the first rags-to-riches success story in American literature. In it, Franklin tells of his efforts to achieve "moral perfection," which is no piddling goal.

In addition to inventing bifocals,[1] Franklin was an authority on women, learning a good deal while he was in Paris as Minister to France and writing essays collected as *The All-Embracing Doctor Franklin.*

THOMAS PAINE

Paine championed the independence of the colonies in a pamphlet entitled *Common Sense.* Since some feared that war against England would be costly and might even mean going into debt, Paine cried fervently, "No nation ought to be without a debt!"[2] Washington ordered Paine's *The Crisis* read to his troops at Valley Forge, particularly the bit about the "summer soldier and the sunshine patriot," which gave his men, stamping around in the snow and blowing on their fingers, a nice warm feeling.

REVOLUTIONARY SONGS AND BALLADS

The songs and ballads of the Revolution threw a scare into the British, causing them to show the whites of their eyes at Bunker Hill.

---

[1] It is said that he "wrote always with his eye on his audience," and the eyestrain must have forced him to desperate measures.

[2] Tom Paine, thou should'st be living at this hour.

PHILIP FRENEAU

"With Freneau," says one critic while Anne Bradstreet turns over in her grave, "American poetry begins." Speaking of graves, one of Freneau's best-known poems is "The Indian Burying Ground," in which he describes the Indian custom of burying their dead sitting up instead of lying down. The deceased,

> His bow, for action ready bent,
> And arrow, with a head of stone,

was on the alert, ready for anything.

THE HARTFORD WITS

The Hartford Wits, also called Connecticut Pranksters, included John Barlow, who won his reputation as a wit with his poem, *The Hasty-Pudding*, describing a dessert that can be prepared in half the time it takes to read about it. At the end of the poem, Barlow is so sure he has the reader drooling that he says, "Fear not to slaver, 'tis no deadly sin," and hands him a napkin.

THE EARLY NOVEL

The first full-length novel written in America by an American was *The Power of Sympathy*, which was published anonymously in 1789. Being about illicit love affairs, a narrow escape from incest, and suicide, it got the American novel off to a good start.

The tradition was carried on by Charles Brockden Brown, who is remembered chiefly for *Wieland*, a novel in which Wieland is driven insane and urged by a ventriloquist to murder his wife and children and does.[1] On behalf of the ventriloquist, a chap named Carwin, it must be said that he also persuades Wieland, who had escaped from a lunatic asylum, not to kill his sister but to do something humane, for once, and stab himself.

EARLY DRAMA

The first comedy was *The Contrast,* written in 1787 by Royall Tyler. The contrast in *The Constrast* is between a two-fisted, patriotic American and a one-fisted, unpatriotic Anglophile. When *The Contrast* was played in Boston in 1792, it was advertised as "A Moral Lecture in Five Parts." Bostonians who sneaked in, knowing it was really a play, were careful not to laugh.

WILLIAM DUNLAP

William Dunlap's discovery that a living could be made out of writing plays had a profound influence on the course of American drama. More people took up writing drama as a way of making a living and starved to death.[2]

WIDENING HORIZONS

We now come to a period of widening horizons. Every morning people would rush outdoors to look. "A little wider today, don't you think?" they would ask each other hopefully.

WASHINGTON IRVING

In his *Knickerbocker's History of New York* Irving

---

[1] That last word is a verb. He did not kill any female deer.
[2] What many of these dramatists did not know was that Dunlap managed the leading company of actors and owned the theater in which his plays were produced.

116

wrote of the days when New York was not New York but New Amsterdam and when "every woman stayed at home, read the Bible, and wore pockets." Those were happy times. Another of his works, *The Sketch Book,* surprised many purchasers who opened it expecting to find drawings and were sadly disappointed. They did, however, find some of the first American short stories. One of these is "Rip Van Winkle," about a man who slept for twenty years, which is the equivalent of getting his eight hours 21,900 times.[1] He awoke feeling rested.

THE EXPANDING FRONTIER

About the same time the horizon was widening, the frontier was expanding. America was on the move, and Americans had to be quick about it, or they would be left behind as the rivers and mountains rushed past them.

JAMES FENIMORE COOPER

Anyone who has ever read Cooper's *The Last of the Mohicans* will never forget Chingachgook (no relation to Gobbledygook) and his son Uncas, or the way people were always being aroused to danger by the breaking of a twig. Then there is that great scene where an evil Huron (Bad Indian) "sheathes his knife in the bosom of Cora," and his chief, the still more evil Magua, leaps upon Uncas and "passes his knife into his bosom three several times." What with the killing of Cora's killer by Uncas and the killing of Uncas's killer by Hawkeye, hardly a bosom was left unperforated.

Time and again Cooper proved himself a master at depicting the vanishing Indian—one moment in clear view

---

[1] Or, allowing for five leap years, 21,915 times.

and the next, before you could draw a bead on him,[1] out of sight in the bushes.

WILLIAM CULLEN BRYANT

Bryant was morbid from an early age. In "Thanatopsis," written when he was a teen-ager, he eagerly looked forward to the day when he would "mix forever with the elements" and be "a brother to th' insensible rock and to the sluggish clod." The only trouble with having a rock and a clod in the family, brothers under the soil, was the chance of being run down by a plowshare or tickled by a growing root. It was likely to be a little crowded down there.

He was also a nature lover. In "The Yellow Violet" he says, "Sweet flower, I love, in forest bare, to meet thee," and one gets a striking picture of Bryant, stark naked, running through the woods, hands outstretched, and the shrinking violet shrinking.

THE TRANSCENDENTALISTS

The Transcendentalists established Brook Farm, a socialistic community where agriculture and the arts mingled, it being common practice to milk a cow with one hand while painting a landscape or writing a poem with the other. Mostly, however, unpleasant chores were assigned to a committee and forgotten, life being so beautiful that everyone was too busy looking at it to work.

RALPH WALDO EMERSON

Emerson lived in a house that had been built for his grandfather and was therefore referred to as "the Old

---

[1] Why you should want to draw a bead on an Indian, already weighted down by real beads, I fail to understand.

Man's."[1] He was a preacher for a while, and even after he left the pulpit continued preaching, as anyone knows who has read his essays.

He has been described as "a deep-seated genius." It might be kinder to say something about his Over-Soul, which may have been big and baggy but didn't show.[2]

Anyone who has difficulty understanding Emerson will be helped by the following explanation: "The Kantian tripartition supplied the epistemological terminology for Emersonian transcendentalism." Suddenly it all becomes clear.

HENRY DAVID THOREAU

Henry David Thoreau's name at first was David Henry Thoreau, but apparently he got himself mixed up.

He built himself a cabin on the shores of Walden Pond, near Concord, at a cost of $28.12½.[3] At least that is what he told the county tax assessor when he came to appraise the place. Out of his experiences Thoreau wrote *Walden*, which hymns the pleasures of being alone with nature—away from newspapers, telephones, and Ralph Waldo Emerson. "If the bell rings, why should we run?" asks Thoreau. Callers who knocked on the door of his cabin often went away, thinking he was not home. Actually, he was getting out of his chair, but slowly.

EDGAR ALLAN POE

There were several rules about writing poetry which Poe admired and followed faithfully, since they were his own.

---

[1] Mistakenly referred to today as the Old Manse.
[2] Or did it? Emerson himself refers to the Over-Soul as "the lap of immense intelligence."
[3] Thoreau not only cut corners, he cut pennies. His cabin had no plumbing, but there were woods all around.

One was that a poem should be about the death of a beautiful woman. Since Poe's women, especially those with names like Lenore and Ulalume, were usually sickening by the second stanza, they were dead before there was time to summon a physician.

In Poe's stories someone is always hiding a body or burying the victim alive. Any well-appointed home, such as that of Roderick Usher in "The Fall of the House of Usher," is as sure to have a vault or a catacomb as a guest bedroom or a second bath, and there is always a spare coffin in the hall closet.

Poe is usually considered gloomy and humorless. But we must not overlook a delightful scene in "The Tell-Tale Heart." The murderer having cut off the head, arms, and legs of his victim preparatory to burying him under the floor, you would suppose the place might be a mite messy. But no. As Poe tells us, "There was nothing to wash out— no stain of any kind—no blood-spot whatever. I had been too wary for that. A tub had caught it all—ha! ha!" The reader, relieved, joins in the laughter.

NATHANIEL HAWTHORNE

For fourteen years, Hawthorne hid away in a solitary chamber under the eaves in the family home in Salem. Emerging at last, "I relied for support on my pen," he tells us, no doubt very stooped and weak. His favorite story was *Pilgrim's Progress,* and he kept reading over and over the part about the Slough of Despond. "I wish I had thought of that," he sighed.

Hawthorne was against sin. Without it, though, he would never have become a great author.[1]

---

[1] If you wish to know more about Hawthorne, especially *The Scarlet Letter,* see the next chapter.

AMERICAN POETRY COMES OF AGE

In the mid-nineteenth century, American poetry came of age. Since more than two hundred years had passed since the *Bay Psalm Book,* this is a striking instance of slow maturation. Even then, traces of childishness lingered.

HENRY WADSWORTH LONGFELLOW

A contemporary describes Longfellow as "sitting by the fireside writing verse on his knee with his eyes closed." It is assumed that he wrote only his shorter lyrics on his knee, saving his thigh and larger areas for such poems as *Evangeline* and *Hiawatha.* And why did he keep his eyes closed? No doubt so he would not have to read what he had just written.

The Courtship of Miles Standish sold 25,000 copies in a single week, a rate that has been equaled only by such literary works as *Fannie Farmer's Cookbook.*[1] *Hiawatha,* which popularized Trochaic Tetrameters,[2] tells of the love of Hiawatha for Minnehaha. Hiawatha showed admirable restraint in not sometimes saying Minnehahahaha and winding up with a bad case of hysterics.

Who does not know the opening line of many of Longfellow's poems? Before answering that question, here is another. Who knows the rest of the poem? To help those who have trouble getting any further, we offer not only a memorable line but one that follows which, if not Longfellow's, will serve the purpose:

---

[1] Someone may yet write a poem entitled *The Courtship of Henry Wadsworth Longfellow,* describing Longfellow's seven-year effort to win his second wife, a courtship of truly epic proportions.
[2] A metrical form, not a cough drop.

The shades of night were falling fast,
And Peeping Toms were foiled at last.

And another:

Under a spreading chestnut tree
Were rusty cans and such debris.

JOHN GREENLEAF WHITTIER

Whittier was a "fighting Quaker,"[1] gritting his teeth and clenching his fists whenever he saw a Social Injustice. At the very thought of slavery, Whittier would go into a frenzy and take violent action, such as writing a poem.

The most famous of Whittier's poems is *Snow-Bound*. Whittier wrote this poem, as most others, in a simple, direct way, unaware of the importance of symbolism and hidden meanings which might have made him a Great Poet or at least the subject of articles in the learned journals. It was of Maud Muller, however, that he wrote probably the sexiest lines in any of his poetry, pruriently referring to her graceful ankles and long-lashed hazel eyes. This was in 1854, at the height of the Victorian period, and it is a wonder the poem was not banned for its anatomical frankness.

OLIVER WENDELL HOLMES

Oliver Wendell Holmes was a New England Brahman, and is not to be confused with an East Indian Brahman, which has short horns and a large hump over the shoulders.[2] Out of his experience as a surgeon came *Old Iron-*

---

[1] The same as a "militant pacifist."
[2] Also known, by cattle fanciers, as a zebu.

sides, about a patient on whom he broke several expensive scalpels before making an incision.

The playfulness of Holmes is indicated by the opening lines of *My Aunt:*

> My aunt! my dear unmarried aunt!
> Long years have o'er her flown;
> Yet still she strains the aching clasp
> That binds her virgin zone.

Some readers have been disappointed, as they read on, to discover that Holmes was not referring to a chastity belt but to a corset.

JAMES RUSSELL LOWELL

A Harvard graduate and editor of the *Atlantic Monthly,* Lowell must have found it difficult to write like an illiterate oaf, but as this passage from *The Biglow Papers* indicates he made a commendable effort:

> He was six foot o' man, A 1,
> Clear grit and human natur',
> None couldn't quicker pitch a ton
> Nor dror a furrer straighter.

When his wife died, Lowell stopped writing poetry. Many think he had done it, all those years, just to annoy her.

HERMAN MELVILLE

Melville's first experience with the sea came as a young man of twenty, when he shipped before the mast to England. The mast arrived a week later. Two years later he went on a whaling voyage to the Pacific. He fled the natives when he discovered where their meat supply came from and heard them talking about New York cuts. A New Yorker himself, he didn't like the way his hosts kept feeling his ribs.

Few works have been so subject to interpretation as Melville's *Moby Dick.* There are those who see *Moby Dick* as an allegory symbolizing the struggle between man and nature. Others, however, find it a thinly veiled epic of seasickness.

WALT WHITMAN

Many questions have been raised about Walt Whitman. One, which we are happy to be able to answer, is: Was his first name Walt or was it really Walter? It was Walter.[1] As young Walt intimates in "Out of the Cradle Endlessly Rocking," he thought his parents were going to treat him like a baby forever. But finally, during the Civil War, he became a male nurse in a Washington hospital. To wounded soldiers, who had dreamt about the beautiful nurses who would care for them during their recuperation, Walt was something of a disappointment. Some of them even refused to let him take their pulse.

Whitman's most famous book of poems was *Leaves of Grass.* Among the poems in it is "Song of Myself." It held up publication of the book for several days, until the printer could get a new supply of type, having run out of the letter "I."

MARK TWAIN

Mark Twain, familiarly known as Samuel Langhorne Clemens, made a name for himself[2] with his story, "The

---

[1] But just try referring to the American poet Walter Whitman and see the looks you get.

[2] That is, Mark Twain. He got the idea from the cry of riverboat men. Why they cried when they said "Mark Twain" is too complicated to go into here.

Celebrated Jumping Frog of Calaveras County." He also made a name for the frog—Dan'l.

His *1601: Conversation as It Was by the Fireside in the Time of the Tudors* is full of Elizabethan language. Being Elizabethan rather than modern, it is not dirty but earthy, an important distinction. Many of Mark Twain's friends considered it coarse and vulgar and asked for extra copies.

In *Tom Sawyer,* Tom makes whitewashing a fence so appealing that other boys pay him for the privilege. As those who have tried this since have discovered, too many other boys have read *Tom Sawyer.* In *Huckleberry Finn,* Huck says such things as "There warn't no home like a raft. Other places do seem so cramped up and smothery, but a raft don't." Huck, who was always sneaking off to go fishing, never stayed in school long enough to learn grammar. By proving how well he could get along without it, he set American education back fifty years.

EMILY DICKINSON

A recluse, Emily Dickinson kept to her room, illegibly scribbling poems on the backs of envelopes and tiny scraps of paper, in a fiendish effort to make things difficult for her editors.

In her poems, she has a way of asking the reader some disconcertingly frank questions. For instance:

Have you got a brook in your little heart,
Where bashful flowers blow?[1]

Another, which we blush to quote, especially since it comes from a spinster, is:

---

[1] An electrocardiogram ought to give the answer.

Did the harebell loose her girdle
To the lover bee?

It is doubtful that Emily ever found out, though she spent many watchful hours in her garden.

One critic, writing of Emily Dickinson, refers to "the artful cricket in her brain." No wonder she stayed in her room all the time.

THE RISE OF REALISM

"During the sixties," says one literary historian, "realism was hovering in the air but refusing to perch." It finally came to rest on William Dean Howells, who was so busy writing he hardly looked up.

WILLIAM DEAN HOWELLS

There is nothing sordid about Howells' realism. In *The Rise of Silas Lapham,* Penelope and Irene, the daughters of Sila Lapham, are so virtuous, so tolerant of their father, and so thoughtful of each other that parents today are tempted to put the book on the fairytale shelf.

Howells once said of the people in his realistic novels, "I turned eagerly to some neutral-tinted person who never had any adventure greater than missing the train to Dedham." What he seems not to have realized is that missing the train to Dedham can be a terrifying experience, especially when it is the last train and means spending the night in Boston. Such a person isn't neutral-tinted, he's as white as a sheet.

HENRY JAMES

One thing that is confusing about the James brothers is

that Henry James wrote psychological novels, while William James wrote novel psychology. Another thing that is confusing is Henry's way of writing. Here is an example from *The Sacred Fount:*

"She's beastly happy?" he broke in getting firmer hold, if not of the real impression he had just been gathering under my eyes, then at least of something he had begun to make out that my argument required. "Well, that *is* the way I see her difference. Her difference, I mean," he added, in his evident wish to work with me, "her difference from her other difference."

Some readers find James hard to follow. It is not true, however, that a reader once wandered back and forth inside a pair of parentheses, unable to extricate himself, until he died of starvation.[1]

AMBROSE BIERCE

Ambrose Bierce made an enviable reputation for saying nasty things about people, especially women, and was widely read, especially by men. In his best-known book, *The Devil's Dictionary,* he defines marriage as "a community consisting of a master, a mistress, and two slaves, making in all, two." Still in this mathematical vein, one of his characteristic epigrams is: "You are not permitted to kill a woman who has injured you, but nothing forbids you to reflect that she is growing older every minute. You are avenged 1440 times a day."[2]

---

[1] It was thirst that got him.
[2] In case you haven't guessed, Bierce was married. His wife referred to him as "my bitter half."

O. HENRY

O. Henry was his pen name, thought up while he was in the pen, serving a term for embezzlement.[1] One of O. Henry's specialties is depicting rundown rooming-houses. In "The Furnished Room," the housekeeper looks like an "unwholesome surfeited worm," and her voice sounds as if it comes from a throat lined with fur. The rug is threadbare and stained, the upholstery is ragged, and the air is foul and tainted. One of the pleasures of reading an O. Henry story is that when you have finished you look around and decide your home isn't so bad after all.

THE RISE OF NATURALISM

Following closely upon the realists came the naturalists, who thought the realists were not realistic enough. American naturalists are supposed to have emulated the French and Russian naturalists, such as E. Zola and I. Turgenev, perhaps hoping to prove that there was just as much drunkenness, crime, lust, and insanity in the United States as in Europe.

STEPHEN CRANE

A sensitive, unorthodox young man, Stephen Crane's first love affair was with an older woman to whom he wrote: "You have the most beautiful arms I ever saw. You never should have to wear dresses with sleeves. If I could keep your arms nothing else would count." This confirmed her worst suspicions, and she fled to England, where she married someone for whom she had more general appeal. Crane recovered and married another, but he

---

[1] His real name, and the one he should have used on his checks, was William Sydney Porter.

frequently dreamt of those well-rounded elbows, gone forever.

His first novel, *Maggie: A Girl of the Streets,* is about a girl who rises from the slums of New York to become a worker in a collar-and-cuff factory and eventually a prostitute. Serious questions about life are raised. For instance, to quote a neighbor in the tenement who hears an uproar in Maggie's room and sticks her head in: "Is yer fader beatin' yer mudder, or yer mudder beatin' yer fader?" With both of these worthies drunk, a third party had to be asked.

Crane won Instant Success with *The Red Badge of Courage,* possibly because many thought it a sequel to *The Scarlet Letter.*

FRANK NORRIS

Frank Norris liked to write of "the raw man, the man with his shirt off, stripped to the buff and fighting for his life." In midwinter, such a man might be fighting just to keep warm. Or, if he had any sense of modesty, he might be trying to get his clothes back. A fine example of one of Norris's heroes is McTeague, in *McTeague.* A muscular dentist with enormous, hairy hands, he pulls out teeth with his thumb and forefinger, thus saving the overhead[1] of expensive dental equipment. The reader gets a close-up view of McTeague at work, right down to "a spot of white caries on the lateral surface of an incisor."

Little Women, published two years before Frank Norris's birth, was one of the most popular books in America during his youth. Its influence on such a novel as *McTeague* is not readily discernible.

---

[1] Or in-the-mouth.

JACK LONDON

The heroes of Jack London's books, such as *The Sea Wolf* and *The Call of the Wild,* are all red-blooded— sometimes red-blooded men and sometimes red-blooded dogs. In *The Call of the Wild* the principal character is a dog named Buck, "the dominant primordial beast," who snarls, shows his fangs,[1] and leaps at someone's throat every few pages. Up in Alaska, where Buck pulls a sled when he isn't ripping open a carelessly exposed jugular, men are men and dogs are wolves. When Buck discovers this latter fact, he joins a wolfpack and lives happily ever after. What a romantic picture he makes, jogging along in the wintry moonlight looking for his evening meal, which is trying to avoid him.

THEODORE DREISER

What upset many good people about Dreiser's *An American Tragedy* was that it flew in the face of the cherished American tradition of Horatio Alger. To get ahead, you were supposed to work hard and save your money and stay away from fast women. Dreiser's Clyde Griffiths drowned his pregnant mistress so he could marry a rich society girl and win wealth and position without working for them. Despite the fact that he was convicted of murder and electrocuted, the story set a lot of people thinking. He almost made it, didn't he? Now if he just hadn't written those letters . . .

Most critics write of Dreiser in superlatives. Ludwig Lewisohn, for example, hails him as "the worst writer of his eminence in the entire history of literature."

---

[1] Should we call them Buck teeth?

NEW DEVELOPMENTS IN POETRY

In our preoccupation with the novel, we have neglected poetry. But then, so has everyone else. However in the second decade of the present century poets learned that although people would not read their poems, they would pay to hear the poet read them. It was not that they wanted to listen to poets but that they wanted to be seen listening to poets. It was Cultural.

VACHEL LINDSAY

One of those who was paid for reading his poems to people was Vachel Lindsay. He emphasized sound. In "The Congo," for instance, notice the emphasis on the third word in the explosive line:

Boom, boom, BOOM![1]

It is in "General William Booth Enters into Heaven" that we find Lindsay at top form in the use of alliteration, as in the opening line, "Booth led boldly with his big bass drum." More nearly complete alliteration might have been achieved had the line read, "Booth bled boldly with his big bass broom."[2]

EDWIN ARLINGTON ROBINSON

"Robinson's life, like his muse," says one critic, "was overshadowed by gloom." He had the peculiar knack of seeing the dark side of everything.

Tilbury Town, of which Robinson wrote with such brilliant despondency, was full of people like Richard Cory, who for no apparent reason, except perhaps to

---

[1] Students are likely to pick this line for memorization.
[2] This makes no sense, but the sound is terrific.

prove his marksmanship, put a bullet through his head; Miniver Cheevy, who had a bad cough that was likely to be the death of him; and Cliff Klingenhagen, who drank wormwood instead of wine.[1] Anyone in Tilbury Town who laughed was probably crazy.

AMY LOWELL AND
EDNA ST. VINCENT MILLAY

Two poets who had much in common were Amy Lowell and Edna St. Vincent Millay. Both were women. But they had their differences, too. For instance, Miss Lowell smoked cigars, while Miss Millay burned her candle at both ends.[2]

Amy Lowell was an Imagist, and wanted her poems to be "hard and clear." This is a confusing statement, because when a poem is hard it isn't clear and when it's clear it isn't hard. Miss Millay, it has been said, wrote with "rapturous intensity." An example is this intense line in her poem "Recuerdo":

And you ate an apple, and I ate a pear.[3]

ROBERT FROST

Robert Frost was born in California, and had he not left there as a boy and lived most of his life in New England, it is hard to imagine his writing books with titles like *North of Boston* and *New Hampshire.*[4] In "Mending Wall" Frost says, "Good fences make good neighbors."

---

[1] Cliff was something of a trial to his friends, who had to keep a bottle of wormwood on hand, just for him.

[2] So far as is known, Miss Lowell never tried this with a cigar.

[3] On second thought, this might better be described as an example of her ravenous intensity. She and her lover were both hungry.

[4] However, he might still have written *Complete Poems.*

Anyone who has built a high fence to keep out a neighbor's destructive children will appreciate the wisdom of this observation.

The range of Frost's poetry is shown by such representative titles as "The Pasture," "The Tuft of Flowers," "Mowing," "Blueberries," and "The Cow in Apple Time." "I wonder about the trees," he says in a haunting line that keeps you wondering.

CARL SANDBURG

Sandburg saw life clearly despite an unruly lock of hair that fell down over his eyes. What he saw is indicated by a passage from his famous poem, "Chicago":

> They tell me you are wicked and I believe them,
>   for I have seen your painted women under
>   the gas lamps luring the farm boys.

That was in 1914, when there were still farm boys and before women learned to use eye shadow correctly and to stand under electric lights.

He was a little uncertain about himself, in various poems saying "I am the people," "I am the prairie," "I am dust," and even "I am a copper wire slung in the air." It is no wonder that one of his poems is entitled "Who Am I?"

F. SCOTT FITZGERALD

F. Scott Fitzgerald was the spokesman of the Jazz Age, when most people were too busy drinking and dancing to say anything. "You tell 'em, Scott," was about all they could mumble before they slipped to the floor in a drunken stupor.

In such novels as *This Side of Paradise* and *The Great Gatsby,* Fitzgerald depicted the spirit of the hour, which was usually about 4:00 A.M. His suave young men, always commuting between Princeton and the Plaza in Stutz Bearcats or Locomobiles,[1] never sat still for long. It was too uncomfortable, with a large flask in the hip pocket.

Wealth fascinated Fitzgerald, who once commented to Ernest Hemingway that he was interested in the very rich because they are somehow different from other people. "Yes," Hemingway said, "they have more money." This had never occurred to Fitzgerald before, and he went right home and told Zelda.

GERTRUDE STEIN

One of Gertrude Stein's most beautiful and plaintive lines is

Pigeons on the grass alas,

which is frequently printed

Pigeons on the grass, alas.

That gratuitous comma between *grass* and *alas* takes much of the sorrow out of the grass, which was in a sad state because of pigeons. This is made clear in what follows:

Short longer grass short longer longer shorter yellow grass Pigeons large pigeons on the shorter longer yellow grass alas pigeons on the grass.[2]

---

[1] Often at speeds as high as fifty miles per hour. One of his characters at the wheel of a Stutz Bearcat had "a half-sneer on his face," the wind apparently having blown off the other half.

[2] In *Four Saints in Three Acts,* shorty before the exciting scene which opens: "Letting pin in letting let in let in in in in let in."

Gertrude Stein's style of writing is said to have been influenced by the brushstrokes in a Cézanne painting that hung over her typewriter.

EZRA POUND

What attracted Ezra Pound to the Imagists was probably the mellifluous and descriptive name of their journal, *Blast*. His *Cantos* influenced T. S. Eliot's *The Waste Land* and depressed countless readers because they thought themselves stupid, not being able to understand.

H. L. MENCKEN

While other critics collected their prejudices in volumes entitled *Literary Criticism,* H. L. Mencken called his prejudices *Prejudices.* As for his guiding principle in life, he summed it up best in his oft-quoted remark: "I've made it a rule never to drink by daylight and never to refuse a drink after dark." It was this sort of wisdom that caused Mencken to become known as The Sage of Baltimore.

SINCLAIR LEWIS

Sinclair Lewis put Sauk Center, Minnesota, on the map.[1] In *Babbitt* he has such wonderfully realistic dialogue as

> "Shall we have the Gunches for our dinner, next week?"
> "Why sure; you bet."

There is a touch of genius about that "you bet," it rings so true to the American vernacular. No wonder Sinclair Lewis won the Nobel Prize.

---

[1] About a hundred miles northwest of Minneapolis.

The main theme of such novels as *Babbitt* and *Arrowsmith* is that money does not pay. In *Main Street, Elmer Gantry,* and other works Lewis "laid bare the materialism, hypocrisy, and self-seeking of Americans," who loved it. The only writers who have made more money out of showing up Americans for what they are have been British.

CONTEMPORARY DRAMA

In the twentieth century, American dramatists began to throw off the shackles of convention. Sometimes a dramatist threw a shackle too far and it hit a theatergoer in the third row center.

EUGENE O'NEILL

O'Neill, a handsome, brooding man, had "an eye that turned inward," which must have been annoying. He left his second wife and children to run off with an actress, tried to commit suicide, and felt most at home in a saloon called the Hell Hole. After reading a biography of O'Neill, one not only understands his tragedies better but finds them a relief.

It was O'Neill's contention that man is doomed and there is no escape—he is doomed if he does and doomed if he doesn't. A few lucky people die young. Sometimes, as in *Mourning Becomes Electra,* O'Neill goes to the classical writers for his material, not finding anything morbid enough in the world around him.

O'Neill's plays are notable for their devices. In *The Great God Brown,* for instance, the characters wear masks, even though it isn't Halloween. Almost as original as the devices in O'Neill's plays are the titles, such as *Desire Under the Elms,* which causes one to envision a fall scene in New England, with a tired leafraker looking up hopelessly, and *The Iceman Cometh,* with its subtle suggestion of a hot summer day and a housewife with a lisp.

A statistician has determined that in O'Neill[1] there are twelve murders, eight suicides, twenty-three other deaths, and seven cases of insanity. No one has had the courage to count the cases of Scotch.

CONTEMPORARY FICTION

In contemporary fiction, especially in the short story, the author gives us a slice of life. Perhaps he is carving out a reputation for himself. Then again, he may be sharpening a pencil and the knife slips. "But," as one critic has said, "no matter how thin you slice it, it is still life."[2]

ERNEST HEMINGWAY

Always interested in sports, Hemingway is said to have worn boxing gloves while typing, which may account for an occasional blurred image. His most celebrated physical encounter was his bout with Max Eastman, who had intimated that Ernest wore a toupee on his chest.

In both *The Sun Also Rises* and *Death in the Afternoon* he writes enthusiastically of bullfighting, there being nothing so beautiful as a bull falling to the ground, blood gushing from his wounds. The fleeting instant the matador and the bull stand eyeball-to-eyeball, just before the matador plunges his sword into the bull or the bull plunges his horns into the matador, Hemingway thought of as the Moment of Truth. What the matador thought we can only guess, perhaps "There must be some easier way to make a living."

In *A Farewell to Arms* and *For Whom the Bell Tolls* Hemingway writes brilliantly of battles, for instance the struggle of Robert Jordan and Maria to get into one

---

[1] In his plays, that is.
[2] Not to be confused with the still life of painting.

sleeping bag. This is a striking change from the romantic, unrealistic literature of earlier days, when a man would doff his hat[1] and give up his sleeping bag to a lady.

We have said nothing of the symbolism of *The Old Man and the Sea*. Could Hemingway have been the Old Man? Everyone called him "Papa."

WILLIAM FAULKNER

Most of Faulkner's novels are set in Yoknapatawpha County, full of hard drinking and hard spelling. The Sartorises are an old Southern family on the way down, while the Snopses are a new Southern family on their way up. Thus they represent the ups and downs of the South. *The Sound and the Fury* introduced another family, the Compsons, who tried to keep up with the Sartorises, never letting them get ahead when it came to lust, incest, and suicide. Somewhat unusual among the Compsons was Benjy, who being a moaning, slobbering idiot was not inclined to forgery and sexual immorality like the rest of the family.[2]

Faulkner was working up to his masterpiece, *Sanctuary*, which has been hailed as "a classic of horror and degradation."

Quite as important as his brilliant picture of the South is his prose style, which includes the technique of "interior monologue." Anyone sitting near a person thus engaged usually supposes it to be a growling stomach and pretends not to notice.[3]

---

[1] And that was all he doffed.

[2] Faulkner was rather partial to idiots. Charles Bon, the idiot in *Absalom, Absalom!*, was about the only person not murdered or burned to death when the old plantation house was set fire to. He merely disappeared, and nobody looked very hard for him.

[3] For some reason, Faulkner's prose is clearer in translation, as anyone knows who has read *As I Lay Dying* in Finnish or Urdu.

Closely associated with his prose style is his symbolism. In *The Sound and the Fury,* for instance, ever time Faulkner mentions honeysuckle the reader can expect something about sex. In fact the reader can expect something about sex even without any mention of honeysuckle. But this has not lessened Faulkner's popularity.

CONCLUSION

American literature did not come to an end with Hemingway and Faulkner, despite rumors to the contrary. The subject matter of contemporary fiction can best be summarized by the title of one of Mailer's novels, *The Naked and the Dead,* which is not, as you might suppose, about the members of a nudist colony having a picnic in a cemetery. Drama has taken on new dimensions with the works of Tennessee Williams and Arthur Miller. In *A Streetcar Named Desire* and *Death of a Salesman* these dramatists achieved the seemingly impossible by being more depressing than O'Neill. As for poetry, it can safely be said that it has come a long way from Anne Bradstreet and the *Bay Psalm Book* to Allen Ginsberg and his *Howl.*[1]

That would seem a good note on which to end.[2]

---

[1] For the source of Ginsberg's howl, see Walt Whitman's "barbaric yawp."
[2] Except for a final footnote.

VIII
American Novel

And now for an American novel. I have two American novels in *The Classics Reclassified*, along with works such as *The Iliad* by non-American but not necessarily un-American authors. The two novels are *The Scarlet Letter* and *Moby Dick*, and space permits me to include only one here.

As an example of an English novel, in an earlier chapter, I chose *David Copperfield* over *Ivanhoe* or *Silas Marner*. The reason I gave was that *Ivanhoe* and *Silas Marner* are not on all the required reading lists these days, as they once were, and I could not be sure my reader had read them. It seemed hardly fair to the author if my version of his (or her) novel were read and not his (or hers). (But for George Eliot, I would not be forced into all these parentheses.)

As for *The Scarlet Letter* and *Moby Dick,* I think both are still on the required reading lists. I hope they are. There is only one American novel that equals or surpasses them, and that is *Huckleberry Finn,* which I have never tried to retell because I marvel that Mark Twain was able to tell it in the first place. But I am here not to praise a novel but to bury it. Not deeply, of course, and only momentarily, because whichever novel I choose is too much alive for permanent burial. It would climb right out and bury the gravedigger.

Both *The Scarlet Letter* and *Moby Dick,* though, have their defects or excesses. In *Moby Dick* it is Melville's penchant for digression. Just as the story gets moving, the author stops it so that he can tell us about all the different types of whales and give us a short history of mastheads, starting with the Egyptians. Later, as the plot thickens, he thins it out with an account of the manufacture of rope lines, the anatomy of the whale's eye, ear, and tail, and how to skin a whale and cook the blubber. For good measure, he throws in the highlights of whaling from Perseus to the present. Captain Ahab, the protagonist of the story, at last makes his appearance (and what an appearance it is!) in Chapter XXVIII, while Moby Dick, after whom the novel is named, doesn't show up until Chapter CXXXIII.

In *The Scarlet Letter* the excess is a preoccupation with sin. This is perfectly proper with such perfectly proper people as the Puritans of New England, but it strikes us, or some of us, as a bit absurd. We have learned to live with sin (and I am making no reference here to my wife) and even to enjoy some minor forms of it without feeling sinful. Beauty, I sometimes think, is only sin deep.

Sin must have been even more fun before Puritan times, in the Middle Ages, when the verb "to sin," which was usually "sinnen," was sometimes spelled "singen." The association of sinning and singing leads to all sorts of interesting possibilities. I have not yet found an etymological connection between sinning, singing, and swinging, much though I should like to. Nor have I heard anyone say, at least not in so many words, "You will have to sin for your supper."

But I am getting away from *The Scarlet Letter.* Or am I? Apparently Hester Prynne and Arthur Dimmesdale and Nathaniel Hawthorne and I are all interested in sin, though perhaps in different ways.

Much as I regret giving up Ahab, Ishmael, Queequeg, and the rest, I have decided to give here my retelling not of *Moby Dick,* with its flukes and fins, but *The Scarlet Letter,* with its flukes and sins. I may even start wearing a scarlet A on my sweater, standing of course for "Armour." Or "Amour," as many mistakenly, but not too mistakenly, call me.

Without further ado, and I apologize for all the ado so far, here is *The Scarlet Letter.*

THE SCARLET LETTER

The story is set in Boston, back in colonial times, when sin was really sinful. Everyone there is a Puritan, since all the other people are either still in England or have gone to Virginia or to hell. The Puritans are a gloomy lot, and by the time the reader gets to the second paragraph, in which the author dwells lovingly on jails and cemeteries, he knows this is no place to be looking for laughs.

As the narrative begins, a crowd has gathered in front of the weather-stained prison door. Growing by the door is a rosebush, and the reader who is alert to such things knows it is a Symbol. Nevertheless, just to be sure, Hawthorne picks one of the roses and explains that this will serve "to symbolize some sweet moral blossom" which, he says, will "relieve the darkening close of a tale of human frailty and sorrow." Hawthorne then presents the rose to the reader, who can either clutch it nervously in his hand while he reads or press it in the book if it is not a library copy.

At last the door of the jail opens, and out comes Hester Prynne, a tall young woman "with a figure of perfect elegance on a large scale." The women among the spectators, all of whom wear petticoats and farthingales and have noses sharp enough to use for letter openers, whisper to each other, hoping Hester can hear. In their humble opinion she is a naughty baggage, a malefactress, and a transgressoress.

What fascinates the onlookers is something embroidered on Hester's bosom or, more accurately, on her dress. It is not only embroidered but illuminated, so that it will be visible by night. This ornament is a SCARLET LETTER. The letter, which the prisoner has fashioned herself with a needle friends smuggled to her in a pincushion, is an "A." Apparently she had intended to go through the alphabet, making a New England sampler, but ran out of thread.

Prodded along by a grim beadle, Hester makes her way to the market place, where she climbs up onto the scaffold, without, however, "undergoing that gripe about the neck and confinement of the head, the proneness to which was the most devilish characteristic of this ugly engine." She has an infant in her arms, and what with this and "the heavy weight of a thousand unrelenting eyes," is really burdened down. There she poses with her chin up for hours, while it gradually dawns on the reader that she has sinned and is being punished.

Some time earlier, it seems, Hester was married in England to a gentleman old enough to be her father, or even grandfather, a man with "a pale, thin, scholar-like visage, and eyes dim and bleared by the lamplight." His left shoulder was higher than his right, which was no help either to his looks or to his tailor. What attracted Hester to him Hawthorne does not explain, probably because he was unable to figure it out himself.

Two years before, Hester's husband had sent her to America, saying he would be along later. But he never arrived. Naturally, she assumed he was dead. How was she to know that he had indeed come to America but had fallen into the hands of Indians, who detained him nearly two years, trying to decide whether, with his thinning hair, he was worth scalping?

After a year or so, Hester had grown tired of waiting and had given birth to a child. There was strong suspicion that she had had an accomplice. But who? Everyone was busy guessing. The suspense was mounting, and so was the anxiety of young men about town, improper Bostonians unable to think up an alibi.

Now, standing on the platform, Hester stares back proudly at the curious Puritans. Suddenly she sees an elderly man whom she recognizes by his "furrowed visage"[1] and by the fact that his left shoulder is a trifle higher than his right. It is her husband! He bends his eyes on her and she fastens hers on him. She clutches her sin-born infant to her heaving bosom until the poor thing is in danger of becoming seasick. Meanwhile her husband's face darkens and "a writhing horror," having "twisted itself across his features," slithers off into the bushes. It gives you the creeps.

Before being returned to prison, Hester is exhorted by the Governor (a political hack who ran on the Puritans First ticket) and other somber dignitaries to confess who is the father of her little bastard. One of the righteous gentlemen who lecture the erring woman is her pastor, the Reverend Arthur Dimmesdale, a nice young clergyman who has large brown melancholy eyes and "a mouth which, unless when he forcibly compressed it, was apt to be tremulous." His mouth is wobbling like jelly when he asks Hester to name her baby's father. Thereupon, lo and behold, her sin-baby lifts up its little arms to the minister so appealingly that one begins to wonder. No, it *couldn't* be!

Back in prison, Hester is visited by her husband, Roger

---

[1] He was run over by a plow.

Chillingworth, a cold fish whose name fits him better than his clothes.

Hester is in a state of nervous excitement, and the child, "who, drawing its sustenance from the maternal bosom, seemed to have drunk in with it all the turmoil, the anguish and despair, which pervaded the mother's system," is sick to its little stomach. Chillingworth opens his leathern case and gives Hester and her baby a draught he learned about from the Indians. Hester quaffs it without even glancing at the label, she is that trusting. No wonder the girl is in trouble.

Chillingworth is no M.D., and has had only a basic course in alchemy. Moreover, his bedside manner leaves much to be desired. Instead of asking Hester how she feels, he asks her who is the father of her child.

"Ask me not!" replies Hester, who is never without an exclamation point. "That thou shalt never know!"

Chillingworth swears he will find her lover. "He bears no letter of infamy wrought into his garment, as thou dost," he hisses, "but I shall read it on his heart." He probably learned how to do this from the Indians, too. Meanwhile Hester must promise not to disclose to anyone that Chillingworth is her husband.

"Breathe not the secret, above all, to the man thou wottest of," says Chillingworth menacingly and then, picking up his leathern case, oozes out. He is up to something, though Hester wots not what.

When her prison term is over, Hester goes to live in a little thatched cottage on the outskirts of town. You'd think she would clear out of there and go to New York or somewhere more congenial to sin. But no, she stubbornly sticks around, for the good of her soul and Hawthorne's plot. She makes her living plying her needle, with which she is so felicitously diligent that she makes no distinction between work and ply.

Always she wears a scarlet letter on her blouse. Research has failed to reveal exactly how she managed it. Did she have one special blouse for show, so to speak, with a scarlet letter on it? Did she have half a dozen blouses, each with its letter? Or did she have one letter, which was detachable and could be switched from blouse to blouse? This is the sort of problem that makes literary scholarship so fascinating.

With Hester lives her child, named Pearl.[1] As time passes, she grows into a difficult little girl who is forever asking her mother embarrassing questions about the scarlet letter. As Freud could have told Hester in a minute,[2] her daughter is clearly manifesting a latent consciousness of sex. Townspeople think Hester a bad influence, and the Governor, who seems to have no more important state business, is about to take Pearl from her mother when the Reverend Mr. Dimmesdale intervenes, his mouth wobbling like mad. Henceforth he clutches his heart each time he speaks, and one need not be a cardiologist to know that the old ticker cannot stand this sort of mauling for long.

Meanwhile Roger Chillingworth, the wronged husband, remains in town, setting himself up as a physician without a license. His professional services are welcomed, because the only other surgeon is the local barber, who can start a flow of blood but has difficulty stopping it. Chillingworth's favorite patient is the sickening Mr. Dimmesdale,[3] who is getting paler and thinner every day, in part because of his practice of fasting "to keep the grossness of his earthly state from clogging and obscuring his spiritual lamp."[4]

---

[1] Perhaps because she is slightly unstrung.
[2] Though, to justify his fee, he would have taken considerably longer.
[3] There are some who think Dimmesdale absolutely nauseating.
[4] What he needs is a new wick.

Since he continues to decline, "Doc" Chillingworth applies leeches to his veins, where they slurp away merrily. Poor Mr. Dimmesdale fails to become more robust, but the leeches grow so fat they can hardly waddle off to the next patient.

Chillingworth now moves in with the young preacher, not merely to save house calls but to make it possible for him "to go deep into his patient's bosom, delving among his principles, prying into his recollections, and probing everything with a cautious touch, like a treasure-seeker in a dark cavern." Sigmund Chillingworth may have no medical degree, but all that time he claims to have spent with the Indians he was probably in Vienna.

In short, Chillingworth is beginning to think Mr. Dimmesdale is his man. One day, coming on the preacher while he is napping, he unbuttons the fellow's vestments and takes a look at his chest. Hawthorne does not tell us what he saw that caused such a wild expression of wonder, horror, and joy. Mayhap his patient's id, for which he had been groping these many weeks, had surfaced for air. At any rate, he is convinced that (1) the Reverend Mr. Dimmesdale is Pearl's father and (2) perseverance pays.

Now, without letting him know he knows, Chillingworth gives his patient the full treatment. This includes feeding him vitamin-rich weeds he picks from the tops of graves. Mr. Dimmesdale, responding encouragingly, gets worse and worse. He takes to looking at himself in the mirror under a green light. He also lashes himself across the shoulders with a bloody scourge he keeps in his bloody scourge closet. When the weather is thoroughly foul, he goes for a walk all unbuttoned.

One particularly ugly night Mr. Dimmesdale goes walking in strange company. He is pushed along by Remorse and pulled back by her sister, Cowardice, probably a couple of tipsy parishioners. Suddenly he finds himself at the foot of the scaffold on which Hester earlier had displayed her red badge, discouraged. Mounting it, he vows to confess his sin at last, knowing full well that it is too dark for anybody to see him and that the townspeople have been in bed since 9 P.M.

Beastly night as it is, Hester and Pearl just happen by, and Mr. Dimmesdale invites them up onto the platform. There they join hands in a circle and make a pretty family picture, a fine example of Togetherness.

"Wilt thou stand here with Mother and me, tomorrow noontide?" inquires Pearl with her usual knack for asking embarrassing questions.

"Nay, not so, my little Pearl," replies the minister, who is inclined to procrastinate. He suggests a somewhat later date, such as Judgment Day.

About this time there is a meteor flash, and Mr. Dimmesdale thinks he sees a great scarlet A in the sky.[1] He may only be imagining things. However, he actually does see Roger Chillingworth, who all the while has been lurking in the bushes with pad and pencil. Chillingworth, a combination roving reporter and house detective, is always on hand when anything interesting happens. He was even in the closet when Mr. Dimmesdale was whipping himself, hiding behind a pile of surplus surplices.

But Mr. Dimmesdale's secret shame is still not revealed to the public. Chillingworth, who fancies himself a sort of colonial Marquis de Sade, wants to torture the sinner for a while. Thus seven years pass, with no more than the turn of a page. Hester is becoming tolerated locally. People have got so they even say "Howdy, thou" to her, but she puts her finger to her lips and points to her bosom. Far from being ashamed, she seems proud.[2]

---

[1] It was a red-letter night.
[2] Of which, the letter or her bosom, Hawthorne does not make clear.

While Hester has been getting almost unbearably saintly, Chillingworth has turned into a devil. "There came a glare of red light out of his eyes," Hawthorne says. Hester goes to him and begs him to stop persecuting Mr. Dimmesdale. Look what it is doing to his own bloodshot eyes. But Chillingworth laughs ("Ha! ha!") in her face. He is enjoying himself. However, Mr. Dimmesdale has run out of laughs, now even scourging himself listlessly.

All this time Hester, who is better than most women about keeping a secret, has not told Mr. Dimmesdale that Roger Chillingworth is her wronged husband. But one day, meeting the minister in the woods, she tells him, and he is taken aback aplenty. His physician! His roommate! Come to think of it, the fellow *has* been acting a little odd, chuckling in that pleased way every time his patient has a heart attack.

After seven years, Mr. Dimmesdale decides he has had it. A ship for England is in harbor, and he and Hester and Pearl will flee to the Old World and start life anew. He begins to pack his vestments, and Hester fills a suitcase with needles.

It looks as if they are to escape. While Hester is happily planning to toss the Scarlet Letter into the ocean, Mr. Dimmesdale, in a burst of enthusiasm and fellowship, has the impulse to tell one of his parishioners a dirty joke. Unfortunately the impulse passes before he can think of one.

Now, alas, Hester learns from the shipmaster that he has booked another passenger for the voyage, one Chillingworth, Roger! This, we must agree, is a tough break. Of course they might drop Roger over the side in mid-ocean, along with the Scarlet Letter, but such a sensible solution does not come to mind. They can think only of dinner at the captain's table, or their morning constitutional around the deck, or a game of quoits or shuffleboard—with Chillingworth's demonic cackle in their ears and his bright red eyes peering from behind a life raft.

Fortunately, there is one way to get out of this apparent impasse, and Hawthorne takes it. As Mr. Dimmesdale strolls through the market place, receiving the congratulations of the townspeople on one of his most hypocritical sermons, he sees Hester and Pearl standing by the very scaffold on which they had stood in shame a couple of hundred pages back. Seized by an impulse,[1] he mounts the platform, signaling them to join him. And who climbs up there with them, uninvited as usual? None other than Chillingworth, Roger!

The Reverend Mr. Dimmesdale now confesses. To wit, he sinned just one little sin, and look at all the trouble he caused. Thereupon he drops dead, but not before tearing open his shirt to bare his chest, on which some of the spectators later testify to having seen a SCARLET LETTER, exactly like Hester's! As to how it got there, opinions vary. A plausible theory is that it was caused by "the ever-active tooth of remorse, gnawing from the inmost heart outwardly," a little like a gopher. Then again it may only have been a rash.

After Mr. Dimmesdale's confession and demise, Chillingworth, having lost his only patient, gives up his medical practice. Gradually he shrivels up and, within the year, expires, or blows away. Hester disappears from the colony for a while, but eventually comes back and spends the rest of her life Doing Good. She continues to wear the scarlet letter on her bosom, but now instead of a stigma it has become a tourist attraction.

When Hester dies, she is buried in the graveyard, where a single tombstone suffices for her and for Mr. Dimmesdale. With admirable succinctness, the only engraving on it is the letter A. We would fain commend such New England thrift.

---

[1] Hawthorne's—to end the novel.

IX
The Human Side

Once upon a time (which is the way you start stories that are hard to believe) I received an extraordinary letter from a former colleague of mine. We had been in the English Department of a certain college for several years, and I had disliked the fellow from the beginning. It may have been because he was younger and handsomer and smarter than I. Or, as I prefer to think, it was because he was loud and brash and cocky and contemptuous of those less well endowed physically and mentally.

About six months after I left for a position elsewhere, partly to get away from this abrasive colleague, I received a letter from him. After a few pleasantries, which he must have found difficult, he came to the point. He said he had heard that I didn't like him. I replied, after a few pleasantries of my own, that what he had heard was correct. That was the end of an interesting but brief correspondence.

It was an unusual experience and one I shall always cherish. He is the only person who has ever written me that suspected I didn't like him. Perhaps you have to be in the field of English to encounter people with such frankness, along with other qualities.

My reason for disclosing this incident is that I should like to say something, in this final chapter, about the human side of teaching. The student-teacher relationship is by far the most important, but the relationship of teacher to teacher and teacher to administrator can make life pleasant or make it unbearable. As I have said, I left one institution (an educational institution, not the kind they lock you up in) partly because of an objectionable colleague. I left another place partly because of an objectionable administrator. I shall not go into the details about this second departure, because I do not wish to open a wound that took a long time healing. The wound, I hasten to add, was on me and not on the administrator, a person with too tough a hide to be wounded. Such a hide is, after all, a requirement for anyone thinking of going into college or school administration, just as it is for anyone going into politics, lion taming, or professional wrestling.

I was, I must confess, a Dean of the Faculty for a time, and despite my inordinately thin skin I enjoyed it. When I became Dean, I lost no time assuring the faculty that I was "Dean of the faculty, by the faculty, and for the faculty, so that the faculty shall not perish." As I told them this I tried to look like Lincoln, but needed a tall hat, a scarf, and about six inches more height to make the resemblance convincing.

I had already looked up the word "dean" and discovered that it comes from the Latin *decem,* ten, because a dean, or *decanus,* was originally the chief of ten monks in a monastery. I was the chief of more than ten faculty members, and not a one of them was very monkish or, for that matter, nunnish. Perhaps that was why I got along pretty well with them, because I am not very monkish or nunnish myself.

Here is a slightly tear-stained portrait which may have a little of me in it, along with a recollection of Milton in the opening line:

DEAN OF THE FACULTY

When he considers how his days are spent
(More than professor, not quite president,
Though toward the latter tentatively reaching),
He wonders if he should have left his teaching.
Of course—he rubs his high, impressive brow—
He has a private secretary now
And sits upon the platform in the spring,
Crown prince and heir apparent, though not
    king.
And while some whisper that it must be four,
He really makes a good two thousand more
From what is called the administrative racket
Than any in the full professor bracket.

And yet, with summer just ahead, he dreams
Of bygone days—how one month hardly seems
Enough (as three months did) for going places.
He longs, too, for those rows of student faces,
More cheerful than committeemen. (You know,
The Dean is always *ex officio*.)
He notices the dust that thickens on
The box of three-by-fives. He has not gone
Inside to add a note on Chaucer's -*e*,
Last chapter of his book, since '53.

So he considers how his days are spent,
More than professor, not quite president.

    Even before becoming Dean, I had looked up the word
"curriculum," which is a basic word in the world of administrators, teachers, and students, though only vaguely
familiar to trustees and members of school boards. My
propensity for looking up words led me to write *A Diabolical Dictionary of Education,* in which this definition may
be found:

155

Curriculum. From the Latin *curriculum,* a racecourse or a chariot, which in turn comes from *currere,* to run. From this we also have the curricle, a two-wheeled chaise drawn by two horses abreast. As it is used today, curriculum refers to the body of courses offered by an educational institution, but the original meaning has not been entirely lost. Teachers involved in a curriculum have the feeling of running around and around a race track but never getting anywhere. Some, after a hard day, feel as if they have been pulling a curricle, with the superintendent, principal, and two members of the School Board inside, urging them on.

Applied to the college or university rather than school level, the passengers in the curricle, pulled by an assistant professor, are the president, dean of the faculty, and head of the department. If a trustee were added, the load would be impossible.

I have nothing specifically about English in my educational (to some) dictionary but a good deal about the non-English or semi-English used by many persons, especially administrators, in the field of Education. Educationese, as I point out, has certain basic principles. One is that a short word is never used if a long word is available. Another is that if a long word is not available one can be invented. Still another is that anything that is understandable at first reading needs to be revised. In connection with Business English, which at best might be considered a dialect, I have this footnote: "The efforts of Chinese merchants to pronounce 'business' gave rise to the word 'pidgin.' Business English is therefore, in a way, pidgin English, which will come as no surprise to anyone who has ever studied or taught it."

Mostly, in my dictionary, which runs the gamut (*gamma* plus *ut*) from nursery school to graduate school, I am concerned not with things but with people: trustees, members of the school board, alumni, presidents, deans (all varieties), superintendents, principals, vice principals, department heads, librarians, registrars, directors of admission, directors of development, dietitions, house mothers, counselors, coaches, custodians, and—let us not forget them entirely—students.

The same is true in *Going Around in Academic Circles,* which concentrates on higher education, is in effect a parody of a college catalogue, and is dedicated "To Socrates, the first professor to drink himself to death." The broader scope of *A Diabolical Dictionary* is revealed by its being dedicated "To teaching, the second-oldest profession." Oddly enough, an increasing number of students don't know what the oldest profession was. If they have not been taught such fundamentals, that is the fault of teachers of sociology, or of history, not of English. Teachers of English should not be blamed for all educational lacunae. (An interesting word, "lacuna," from the same Latin root as "lagoon.")

After serving in the English Department, or Department of English if you prefer, of seven institutions, I came to realize that it is in the department that personalities impinge on personalities, and friendships and emnities flower. A department is a political unit, perhaps at the ward level, and the department head is the Boss. Here is my definition:

> *Department.* Actually a compartment, within which is confined all the teaching of a subject as well as all the learning of it, if any. A department may have a rotating chairman (spinning dizzily) or a head. A department head is not to

be confused with the lavatory restricted to members of the department, each of whom has a key which he wears on a chain instead of a Phi Beta Kappa key. The main purpose of a department is to have more majors and a larger book budget than any other department and to keep the knowledge of one field from seeping into another, thus creating a situation that would be dangerously interdepartmental. It might be interesting to imagine Socrates, Erasmus, or Leonardo da Vinci in a department, perhaps in the same department, arguing about credits, prerequisites, and secretarial assistance.

After writing this, I discovered that the word "department" also has the meaning, now obsolete, of "departure." For those on the way out because of a feud within the department, this may have a certain poignancy.

I have mentioned the department head above, but further meditation about this academic character causes me to wax, or perhaps wane, poetic:

DEPARTMENT HEAD

He counts the majors in his field
And checks his closest rival.
More majors mean more funds for books,
More staff, more awed, respectful looks,
Or anyhow survival.

At times he's politic, and then
At times no one's inepter.
But he is always at the helm,
And since he rules his little realm
Should have a crown and scepter.

For many years, my happiest years, I taught in a college where there were no departments. In fact use of the word "department" was forbidden. You would have thought it a four-letter word instead of a ten-letter word. All the fields were put into one or another of five "Courses of Study." One of the five was Literature, which included English, French, German, Spanish, Greek, and Latin. Luckily, English was the language used when we spoke to one another in the hall or met at lunch. The Professor of Classics thought this demeaning, and often said something, such as "Pass the butter, please," in Latin or Greek. He was kind enough to repeat what he had said in English for those who, in his opinion, had never been truly educated. I loved those nondepartmental years, though I was aware that it takes specialization to get ahead.

That brings me to the Publish-or-Perish Syndrome. I was caught in it, and I am rather glad I was. It forced me to write three heavily footnoted books that I might not otherwise have written. I had a collaborator on the third and by far the best of those books, and learned something I wish I had known before. Why write a scholarly book by yourself, with all that research, if you can get just about the same credit in the academic world when someone else does half the work?

Fortunately those books were biographies, and by writing them I learned some things about literature and life, as well as how to find my way around a library. Quite as important, I did not shortchange my students while I was publishing. Teaching came first. I kept my office hours, and more. We frequently invited students to our home. The research and the writing were done *after* everything else—in the evenings, on weekends, during Christmas, Easter, and summer vacations. (Is there any profession with as many vacations as teaching?)

The elementary school teacher, the junior high school

teacher, and the high school teacher are not bothered by Publish-or-Perish. The higher up you go in the academic hierarchy the more it is publication that brings promotion and money and status. Moreover, such publication is likely to be measured quantitatively rather than qualitatively, at least by presidents and deans and those outside the field. And it will probably be read, if read at all, by fellow specialists within a specialty. Once I wrote these lines to describe what all too often happens:

PROFESSOR'S PROGRESS

Each article he wrote, though paper thin
(And thinner still, if truth be known, within),
He placed upon the one he wrote before,
A slowly rising pile upon the floor.
Each tiniest addendum, near ethereal,
Dredged out of desiccated source material,
He placed upon the others there below
And proudly watched the paper pillar grow.
Then mounting quickly with expectant smile
And careful step the scholar's precious pile,
He stood at last triumphant on its tip
And reached, and plucked a full professorship.

Do not mistake me. I am strongly for research and publication, both for making knowledge available and for keeping the professor's mind active and growing. But I doubt that all research has to be published, and I think there are ways to determine mental aliveness and scholarship without counting the titles in a "bibliography."

Still more important, I believe the good teacher should be rewarded fully as much as the good publisher, in those instances when the two are not the same. And who is to determine who is a good teacher? Colleagues, adminstrators—and students. Students should not make the final decision, but they should have a substantial part in supplying the information and judgment on which that decision is based. Students have limited experience. Student opinion can be opinionated. Student evaluation needs to be evaluated. But who knows the nature of the teaching as well as the taught?

A teacher is, after all, a lifetime student, a student who is given respect and money (neither of these sufficient by itself) to keep on studying and to keep ahead of other, younger students but not out of sight.

I shall not go into such matters as tenure and sabbaticals, which are as good conversation pieces among teachers as the weather and the common cold are among others. Well, I might relent a little and point out that the words "tenure" and "tenor" both go back to the Latin *tenere,* to hold. One involves holding a job and the other holding a high note. I have noticed that when arguments concerning tenure become heated, voices are raised.

As for sabbaticals, just as the seventh day of the week is the Sabbath, or day of rest, the seventh year of teaching is a sabbatical, or year of rest. Anyone who is on a sabbatical is well advised to go abroad, where he can rest without being subjected to the envy of colleagues not on a sabbatical. Resting in or near a library or museum is known as doing research.

Throughout this book I have been playful, only occasionally lapsing into seriousness. Now and then I have bared my soul. More often I have bared my feet, because if I stepped on any toes I didn't want to hurt them.

Studying and teaching are, or can be, fun, especially studying and teaching English.

ABOUT THE AUTHOR

Richard Armour, a Harvard Ph.D., has held research fellowships in England and France, has written scholarly books of biography and literary criticism, and has taught for almost forty years in a wide variety of institutions, including the University of Texas, Northwestern University, Wells College, the University of Freiburg, the University of Hawaii, the Claremont Graduate School, and Scripps College, where he was also Dean of the Faculty. In addition, he has lectured or been guest-in-residence on more than two hundred campuses in this country and, as an American Specialist for the State Department, has made five lecture tours that took him to the leading universities of Europe and Asia.

He is best known, however, as a writer of humor and satire in both light verse and prose. He has written for more than two hundred magazines, from *McCall's* to *The Journal of the American Medical Association* and from the *Saturday Review* to *Playboy*. His 47 books are in an incredible number of fields, including not only literature but history, education, sports, medicine, paleontology, war and weaponry, and sex. Among the most popular outside of those in literature are such best sellers as *It All Started with Columbus, It All Started with Eve, Golf Is a Four-Letter Word,* and *Through Darkest Adolescence.* His light verse has been brought together in such books as *Light Armour* and *Nights with Armour,* and his short prose has been collected in *Out of My Mind.* He has also written a dozen books for children, praised by *The New York Times* for their "ingenuity and imagination, fun and excitement."

Richard Armour is married, has a son and daughter, and lives in Claremont, California.